The Rise of Bureaucracy and the Decline of Work – their Roots in the 2nd and 3rd Century Church

MCCD

The Rise of Bureaucracy and the Decline of Work – their Roots in the 2nd and 3rd Century Church

J.D.R. de Raadt

Edited by Veronica D. de Raadt

Melbourne Centre for Community Development

The Rise of Bureaucracy and the Decline of Work
– their Roots in the 2ⁿᵈ and 3ʳᵈ Century Church

Melbourne Centre for Community Development
Australia • 2017

www.melbourneccd.com

Other books by J. D. R de Raadt and Veronica D. de Raadt available for free download at the website above:

Information and Managerial Wisdom

A New Management of Life

Redesign and Management of Communities in Crisis

A Method and Software for Designing Viable Social Systems

Ethics and Sustainable Community Design

Intelligent Christianity for an Age of Folly

*From Multi-Modal Systems Thinking
to Community Development*

All scripture quotations, unless otherwise indicated, are taken from The Revised Version

v3

O GOD... whose service is perfect freedom...

The Book of Common Prayer, Church of England

Table of Contents

Dedication

**To Lieutenant Commander Hernán Hudson Swett
and to the memory of
Second Lieutenant Jorge Holger Miranda
(11/10/1941 – 7/7/2009)
Former Officers of the Chilean Navy**

I have reached that stage in life's journey where most of the road lies behind me and where one can, from this vantage point, take stock of what has been accomplished and to whom one is indebted for this. I have especially thought about my youth and realised how much I received from others and how much I took it for granted. But as I grew older, I became aware of my short-sightedness. Especially I learned to appreciate how important those years were that I spent in the Escuela Naval Arturo Prat, the Chilean Naval Academy. I did not follow a naval career but left the navy as a sub-lieutenant and eventually became a professor. But I know that under my academic gown I have always worn my naval officer's uniform and this helped me enormously to fulfil the scientific and pedagogical work that God assigned me.

In 1961, my first year in the Naval Academy, my divisional officer was First Lieutenant Hernán Hudson and my senior was Jorge Holger, then in his last year before graduation. My last year of training, 1965, was spent mostly at sea and on the sailing ship Esmeralda. Hernán, by then Lieutenant Commander, became my Chief of Studies and Jorge, a Sub-Lieutenant, was in charge of my watch. I am sure this was providential for, especially when one is young, one learns a great deal by imitation and I unconsciously shaped myself as an officer very much by following the lead of these two young men. As anyone would expect, discipline was the daily bread of a naval cadet's life and both Hernán and Jorge were dedicated disciplinarians. But there was a difference, at least in my mind, in the manner they demanded discipline. For in addition to expecting high standards from us, it was also evident that they cared for us and that their expectations were meant to build us up and equip us for the harsh demands of naval life. They certainly built and equipped me for the academic life that was ahead of me.

Hernán was a born teacher. He had the engaging personality to attract one's attention and a wide sphere of interests. In our first year, he taught a class called Professional Orientation, for which I got a distinction. In addition, he regularly addressed us as a group and here he spoke on a variety of topics, which pricked the ears of the future social scientist and philosopher in me. I remember him discussing the historical background of the Vietnam war, the role of President de Gaulle in the restoration of France and the significance of the corridor of Danzig which connected East Prussia with the rest of Germany. But his favourite topic, apart from naval matters, was the family. He especially encouraged us to show regard for the more senior members of our families, not only parents and grandparents, but also uncles and spinster aunts who were often unnoticed by youth. And on social occasions, he required us to dance not only with the young and pretty girls, but also with the more mature matrons whose husbands preferred to sit and argue about politics and such things rather than lead their wives to the dance floor. This was a duty all of us had to share and which we rather irreverently called "towing" – although this expression was used only amongst us. That final year at sea bonded our class to him and won him a special affection that has not waned with the years.

Jorge was a quiet man and behind the typical strictness of a naval officer one soon discovered a deep human warmth. He was humble and unbelievably honest, qualities that often go hand in hand. He had a great gift for listening and empathy and was of enormous help to me when my mother died while we were away in Europe sailing on the Esmeralda. We became close friends; in later years, my living abroad meant we did not see each other very often but, whenever we met, we carried on as if we had only met the day before. We would sit and talk for hours and he always showed great interest in whatever I was doing. When Internet telephony became available we took advantage of keeping in touch more regularly. He died in 2009 and my regret is that he is not with us any longer to read this dedication. I am comforted by the thought that in our last conversation – he in Chile and I in Australia – I had the opportunity to tell him how much I appreciated him as a friend. About ten days later, I received a phone call from his son sadly informing me of his death.

I consider myself blessed in having had these two friends who taught me so much and it is with the greatest of pleasure that I salute Hernán and the memory of Jorge by dedicating this book to them.

Donald

Abbreviations

Gn   Strong's Concordance number (n) for Greek words

Hn   Strong's Concordance number (n) for Hebrew words

LSJ   Liddell, Henry George; Scott Robert; Jones, Henry Stuart. *Lexicon of Classical Greek*

MIC   Mickelson, Jonathan Kristen. *Enhanced Strong's Greek and Hebrew Dictionaries*

MLSJ   Liddell, Henry George; Scott, Robert. *An Intermediate Greek English Lexicon (Abridged)*

NT   New Testament

n.d.   Not dated – this applies mostly to digitalised documents available on the Internet

OT   Old Testament

TWOT   Harris, Laird R.; Archer, Gleason L. and Waltke, Bruce K. *Theological Wordbook of the Old Testament*

Preface

At the beginning of the 2nd century A.D. the leadership of the church was passed on to the Early Fathers who began adapting the Gospel to their own Hellenic culture. Over a period of just one and a half centuries, they converted the communities founded by the apostles into a bureaucracy and their work into worship. They also imported theology from neo-platonism and relegated the natural sciences and the humanities – both essential for work – to secularism. From then on, Christianity became equally ineffective to combat the barbarism of Rome, mediaevalism and now modernity.

This is a study about how the Early Fathers went wrong. Examining their writings is no easy task, but it is necessary so that we should understand their mistakes, for they had long lasting effects that extend to our day. Much of modern individualism, social fragmentation and ambiguity about what it means to be human are rooted in the Hellenic way of thinking that they brought into Christendom.

The book has been written for university students, but it is of interest to anyone concerned about the education of our youth.

1 Introduction

Johannes Vermeer's *The Lacemaker* symbolises the theme of this book and the reason for placing it on the cover. It was painted between 1669 and 1670 at the peak of the golden age of the Dutch Republic. The driving force at the heart of the republic was the philosophy of Christ which touched every corner of Dutch culture including its civic institutions, education, science, architecture, fine arts, trade and not least, care of the needy and vulnerable. The great majority of the work of the Dutch masters was dedicated to portraying this society and its underlying philosophy, and *The Lacemaker* belongs to these. The key to understanding this painting is the place of the Bible on the canvas. It is not in the hands of a preacher, or on a lectern or some other prominent place in a church building. It lays at the lacemaker's right side and very close to her hand. It reminds us of Jeremiah's prophesy that one day God would write his law in the heart of his people including this lacemaker. Here, the Bible lies in between her bobbins, threads and other material the lacemaker uses in her work. I'm sure it is where Christ wished her to have it.

The theme of this painting is Christian work and its dignity. The lacemaker is wearing her best clothes and her hair is neatly combed, expressing both modesty and dignity in her work. Modesty, for she works to serve others; dignity, because all work that serves humanity, no matter how humble, is service to God. The concentration on her work and her gentle enthusiasm in what she is doing conveys both dedication to her task and a sense of freedom. There is no medieval bureaucracy over her dictating how she ought to perform her work. Christ has freed her from it and therefore she assiduously applies herself to her lacework with enjoyment. Apart from her neat attire and the refinement of her manner, the Bible by her side shows that she is an educated woman, for she can read. Reading was, in the 17th century, the great step towards education in Europe and Holland which had, by far, the highest literacy rate on the continent. Many of the Dutch masters' paintings show that Dutch women were educated women. Dutch society recognised the special gifts God had given women and highly valued them. The nimble fingers of a woman could far outdo a man in the speed and accuracy needed for creating intricate patterns of lace. Their talents in domestic duties were also recognised and praised, for home and family were the most revered institutions of the republic. These were not only regarded as building blocks of society but the aim was for the republic itself to be organised as a family[1]. Thus, Vermeer's lacemaker shines with femininity and sweetness. The painting is beautiful because Vermeer has painted the lacemaker as possessing a very special beauty. It is feminine, refined and eager to serve.

Vermeer's vision in *The Lacemaker* represents not only the theme of this book but also the vision my wife and I have endeavoured to pass on to university students. In pursuit of this, we have designed educational programmes to free our students from the grip of neo-liberalism and the bureaucratic machinery that has taken hold of every institution of society, including the university. Few people, not even parents, give much regard to the intellectual and social environment that the contemporary university offers students[2]. It has turned university courses into parcels of "intellectual capital" designed to transform young people into a disposable "human resource" for industry and commerce. But, of even greater concern is university life itself and especially the sexual abuse to which female students are being submitted. In the most extreme cases it involves rape and prostitution[3].

As an alternative to neo-liberalism, we have offered our students the philosophy of Christ that undergirds Vermeer's painting. This philosophy is quite different to the religion the church promotes as Christianity. Christ abolished religion; his

---

[1]   For a study of Pieter de Hooch's paintings of women in their home setting see Lu, 2008.

[2]   J. D. R. de Raadt, 2016

[3]   This is no exaggeration. We have been told about it by students themselves, it has been repeatedly reported in the press, in academic journals and also in an inquiry commissioned by the Australian Senate in 2005. See J. D. R. de Raadt and Veronica D. de Raadt, 2008 and 2014, p. 208.

philosophy[4] was not about transcending this life, but, on the contrary, it was about wisely living it to the full with our feet firmly placed on the earth[5]. We have written extensively about this philosophy as a humane alternative to neo-liberalism[6]. I have now the sad task of explaining how Christ's philosophy was turned into religion, how his kingdom was transformed into a bureaucracy and how work was replaced by worship. This is necessary if we are to encourage young people to follow Christ by tackling the social and cultural chaos before them.

Overview

The analysis of this book is based on social science and philosophy, not on theology. It touches on theological matters only if they have sociological significance. Our first task is therefore to build a model of community that we can use as a template to evaluate the developments that took place in the church in the post-apostolic period. This extends more or less from 100 AD to 250 AD. The model is comprised of five socio-cultural factors that are essential for a community to be viable, free and to develop culturally. These are: goodness, work, familial structure, education and historic vision. These factors are not only identifiable in contemporary society, but were also part of ancient Israel as described in the OT. They played an important role in the emancipation of the Hebrew slaves from Egypt and their formation as a free nation.

Next, we move to the first century and divide the history of the early church into two periods. The first is the apostolic

---

[4]   Since living wisely is the literal pursuit of philosophy, we have followed Erasmus (1529) who defined it as the "philosophy of Christ". In that way, its distinction from theology and the study of religious matters is made clear. Within the systems science literature, I have also referred to it by the more technical term *multi-modal systems thinking*.

[5]   This does not deny eternal life but on the contrary affirms it, for Jesus taught that eternal life is not in the future but now; John 10:28.

[6]   See for example J. D. de Raadt, 2013 and J. D. R. de Raadt and Veronica D. de Raadt, 2014.

period which extends from the baptism of Jesus to the death of the last apostle somewhere at the turn of the first century. The second is the post-apostolic which covers about 150 years. It is during this post-apostolic period that Christ's teachings about the kingdom of God[7] were transformed into a new religion and each of the socio-cultural factors mentioned above was altered according to the following table:

↓	Goodness	Work	Familial Structure	Education	Vision
	Asceticism	Worship	Bureaucracy	Indoctrination	Orthodoxy

The people who produced this transformation – of goodness into asceticism and so on – were the Early Fathers who took over the leadership of the church after the apostles. They played an important role in shaping the theology that has remained unchanged over time and is still part of the mainstream churches of our day – be it Roman Catholic, Eastern Orthodox or Protestant. But, as I have said, we are not interested in theology, but rather in these socio-cultural factors for, in contrast to theology, they, more than theology, determine the everyday life of the laity. Therefore, in Chapters 4 to 11 we examine the writings of each of the most important of these Early Fathers, namely, Ignatius, Justin, Irenaeus, Tertullian, Clement of Alexandria, Origen and Cyprian.

My analysis of their thought – except for Clement of Alexandria – is critical; I especially blame them for having introduced bureaucracy into the church and undermined lay work. However, this is not to say that I do not value them as persons. They were highly talented and educated men who devoted themselves with great sincerity to their scholarly and leadership tasks. And they were prepared to suffer martyrdom for it, which showed the extent of their integrity and that their hearts

---

[7] The kingdom of God has two major dimensions in the NT. The first is general and refers to God's sovereignty of his whole Creation. The second is civic and refers to the rule of God over his people. The theme of this book is mostly concerned with the latter dimension.

were in the right place. We have the luxury of evaluating them using the hindsight of history; they only had the historical times in which they lived. In particular one must consider that, in contrast to the apostles who were solidly reared in the Jewish tradition, these Early Fathers were bred in a Hellenic culture which had a way of thinking that was radically different to the Hebrews. This placed them at a great disadvantage.

Reading the Early Fathers' works is not an easy task and the reader may wonder whether the benefits derived from it justify the intellectual effort required to understand them. May I assure him that they do. It does not help to treat the leaves of a diseased tree when the real problem lies in worms gnawing away the roots; one is obliged to treat the roots. And the roots of many of today's problems are buried in the writings of the Early Fathers. Having pored over their writings for about two years has left me with the impression that the world which they confronted is closer in time than the almost two millenniums that separate us. Humanity does not change much with time and most of the challenges they faced in their time we also face today.

Once this analysis is complete, in Chapter 12 I re-assemble the socio-cultural factors as transformed by the Early Fathers and build a bureaucratic model that represents today's mainstream churches. I then show how neo-liberal bureaucracies have copied this model and added to it a secular ethic based on indulgence and exploitation. This has sent neo-liberalism along a self-destructive path that has disastrous consequences. This same bureaucratic model has impeded the church from arresting the social decline. I then turn to what is known as the emerging church – largely charismatic – and explain how they have organised themselves by copying the neo-liberal model – which is itself a copy of the mainstream bureaucratic model. This has only added fuel to the ravages of neo-liberalism. Thus in Chapter 13, I caution university students about bureaucracies, secular and Christian, and challenge them to dedicate themselves to real work and to rebuilding their communities, helped, I hope, by the scientific contribution we have published in our books and papers.

Finally, as in other writings, I must add a clarification regarding my criticisms of the clergy and theologians. These are directed to their office and not to the good and sacrificial work that many of them perform, thanks to their ability to redefine their work so as to best serve the needs of the people who depend on them. They do this regardless of their job definition and I owe them gratitude and respect for what they do. I have not intended to offend them or to undervalue their worthy contribution. I have plunged ahead with this work for the benefit of young students, for in my role of professor they are my charge and first priority. We must not forget that to them belongs the kingdom of God; they are the future of our society and come first.

2 Goodness and Work

Emancipation and Freedom

If there is one theme that stands out in the Bible as its principal message it is the emancipation of humanity from bondage and oppression – a bondage and oppression that is as much imposed by others as by self. Perhaps, the worst slave is the one who enslaves himself. The main emancipatory event in the OT is the Exodus of the Hebrews from Egypt, where God himself is the liberator, and Moses, his appointed commander to lead the operation. In the NT, both the role of liberator and commander fall on Jesus the Messiah, whose death and resurrection correspond to the OT Exodus. This correspondence is of a reciprocal nature[8], meaning that the effectiveness of the OT Exodus ultimately depended on the death and resurrection of Jesus, while the NT kingdom of God is the ultimate delivery of the land of "milk and honey"[9] promised to the Hebrews. An examination of the measures taken to liberate the Hebrews in the OT reveal some important insights that are relevant to any type of social change aimed at lifting people from their adverse predicament.

Firstly, those engaged in social change should seek to establish a social identity by organising the people immediately into a community and providing the necessary leadership to achieve it. Thus, God chose Moses as a leader who stood before Pharaoh with the request to free not just a number of individuals but his people – his community[10]. Secondly, people ought to be removed from the social environment that has enslaved them and be provided with their own territory to sustain

---

[8] The technical term for this correspondence is *homomorphism*; it denotes a special type of similarity that provides a vital connection between two things that binds them into something more than the sum of its parts. A simple illustration is manhood, which is homomorphic with but not identical to womanhood. This homomorphism allows a man and a woman to become a married couple and share one life and have children.

[9] Exodus 3:8

[10] Exodus 5:1

them and give them an identity. Thus Moses led them out into the desert on the way to the land of "milk and honey".

Thirdly, one must provide the people with a common cultural framework – we may call it a social philosophy – that regulates the whole life of the community and ensures its cohesiveness. People can only both be free and retain their sense of community when they share a common normative framework to regulate their lives. At Mt. Sinai, Israel received from God's own finger the *Torah*. This Hebrew word is commonly translated as *law*, but although it comprised coded statutes that ruled Israel and had thus a civic dimension, it was more than just a law. The word *Torah*[11] literally meant instruction or teaching and it covered a broad scope of understanding[12]. It was the Hebrew approach to philosophy – distinct from the Greek approach – and because it always comprehended life within a social context, we may regard it a social philosophy. But it did not limit itself to human life and society, it also integrated these with nature and served as an intellectual backbone holding all knowledge within a unified whole[13]. In this manner the Torah provided a juridical and civic constitution for its people, as well as serving as a pedagogical instrument to turn them into a civilised community.

Fourthly and finally, one ought to understand that often the worst enemy of a people who are oppressed or in dire circumstances are themselves. Human behaviour in such circumstances resembles the domestic bird in a cage with its door open; it may go out of the cage to have a look around, but soon will return to it where it feels more secure. This is how the Hebrews tended to behave after their liberation; as soon as they faced adversity, they blamed their leader for it and sought to return to Egypt[14]. And finally, when they reached the borders of their promised land, they lacked the pluck to go in and conquer it. They turned back into the desert and were sen-

---

[11]   H8451
[12]   Psalms 19:8; Proverbs 1:2, 6:23, 31:26; 2 Timothy 3:16
[13]   The prototype of a Hebrew philosopher was Solomon whose knowledge spanned from administration to ichthyology (1 Kings 4:30-33).
[14]   Exodus 14:10-12, 16:1-3, 32:9; Numbers 14:1-4

tenced to forty years[15] of wandering in it until all adults – i.e. above twenty years old – had passed away. By the end of the forty year period, the nation was comprised of people with a new mentality. Even though they had been nomads for a long time, they knew freedom and were prepared to fight to keep it. This is sound sociology, for the cycle of social change is one generation. Changes can only begin to be implemented in communities when positions of leadership are assumed by people with a new outlook on life.

Of all these measures, the most important for forming a free community was, without doubt, the giving of the Torah to Israel. The Torah was not just the philosophy that shaped every aspect of life in the nation, but the connecting point between God and his people. Through it, God was physically present in the tablets deposited in the ark of the covenant that eventually occupied the most holy place of the temple[16]. But the Torah delivered at Mount Sinai was only the first instalment of God's revelation necessary to free his people. The second instalment was delivered by Jesus, who was the Torah, God's spoken word[17], now become man and by this was meant "one of us"[18].

There were some changes, however. While in the OT the people received the Torah authored by the Spirit[19], in the NT they received both the Torah and the Spirit, just as the prophets had foretold[20]. Therefore, the physical presence of the Torah shifted out of the temple that had so far housed it and into the inner beings of God's people who became the new temple of his Spirit[21]. This was symbolised by the tearing of the veil that barred the entrance of the people into the holy of the holiest of

---

[15] Numbers 14:28-33, 32:13; Joshua 5:6
[16] Exodus 25:8, 16, 22; 1 Kings 8:6, 9
[17] Exodus 20:1
[18] John 1:1
[19] That is, "the finger of God" (Exodus 31:18; Deuteronomy 9:10; Luke 11:20).
[20] Jeremiah 31:33; Ezekiel 36:26; Joel 2:28-29; 2 Corinthians 3:3; Hebrews 8:10
[21] 1 Corinthians 3:16, 6:19; Ephesians 2:19-22.

the temple[22]. And with the tearing of the veil and the giving of the Holy Spirit at Pentecost, final and complete freedom was granted to the people. Again, we must understand this freedom as being both circumscribed and protected by a social philosophy which was no longer codified in statutes, but that could now be grasped by man's whole intellect with the aid of the Holy Spirit. This philosophy, this wisdom, simultaneously constrained his pattern of living and, at the same time, freed it[23]. At a time when any form of constraint by social norms is seen as an infringement on individual freedom and a violation of our right to do as we please, I would like to make brief reference to my own work in socio-cybernetics[24] that supports the biblical position in this matter. This work has borrowed much from Ashby, who has some important things to say about constraints:

> Constraints are of high importance in cybernetics... because when a constraint exists advantage can usually be taken of it... Constraints are exceedingly common in the world around us, and many of our basic concepts make use of it in an essential way. Consider as an example the basic concept of a "thing" or "object", as something handled in daily life. A chair is a thing because it has coherence, because we can put it on this side of a table or that, because we can carry it around or sit on it. The chair is also a collection of parts... [but] the essence of the chair's being a "thing", a unity, rather than a collection of independent parts corresponds to the presence of the constraint.[25]

What this means, when applied to a community, is that its identity, its unity and its functioning cannot exist without constraints. If one removes them, it will be the same as sitting on a chair with loose legs.

---

[22] Matthew 27:51;
[23] John 8:32
[24] J. D. R. de Raadt, 2015; J. D. R. de Raadt and Veronica D. de Raadt, 2014
[25] Ashby, p. 130f

The giving of the Torah in the person of the Holy Spirit also defined the nature of the New Israel. Its territory was not limited to Canaan, but extended over the whole of the Creation that Christ had claimed as his own[26]; everywhere people set their eyes was now on the land of milk and honey. Therefore instead of God's people having to emigrate, we may say that it was now Pharaoh – the prince of this world – who had to go out into the wilderness[27]. As expected, he fought tooth and nail to hold his ground[28]. This in turn changed the mode of the taking of the land. While in the OT the Israelites fought for their territory and pushed their enemies out of it, now the land of milk and honey was open to all people. Christendom[29] – the New Israel – was a federation of communities overarching all of humanity. A battle still raged; not against flesh and blood but against ignorance and folly, not fought with weapons but with education[30] and the development of a community of free citizens.

Operationalisation

Social scientists use the word *operationalisation* to describe the step necessary to pass from social theory to its application in real life. Like most scientific jargon, it is admittedly an awkward word, yet despite this, it well describes what must be done. The Latin root *opera* means work, operationalisation is an attempt to make a working model to identify, measure or describe things in real life that should correspond to the elements belonging to the theory. Usually, the working model appears more rudimentary than the theory, but that is not a bad

---

[26] Colossians 1:16-20
[27] John 12:31; Luke 10:17-18
[28] 1 Peter 5:8
[29] Defined by the Oxford dictionary as the "worldwide body or society of Christians". I have argued that this is what Christ intended to institute when he used the term *ekklesia*, J. D. R. de Raadt, 2013, p. 83ff. What we call *church* is not the *ekklesia* but a replica of the ancient temple or synagogue, both of which were made obsolete by the Gospel.
[30] 2 Corinthians 10:3-5

thing, as it reflects that theories, when set in front of reality, are often far less sophisticated than the impression they give in the abstract. Here, we need the working model from the Bible's vision of Christendom for two purposes. Firstly, we need it as a tool to evaluate the development of the church over the centuries and to identify where it has done well and where it deviated from the vision that Christ gave his disciples. Secondly, such a model can help us turn things around in order to set things on their proper path again.

How to build the required working models and how to apply them is beyond the scope of this book and has already been dealt with elsewhere[31]; here we need only a few concepts for the task at hand. This involves two steps. Firstly, we must identify a set of factors that are vital to the long term viability and development of a community. To keep our analysis at a manageable level we have limited ourselves to six such factors: (i) a community's goodness, (ii) work, which I shall define below, (iii) its social organisation, (iv) its educational system, (v) its history and (vi) its vision[32]. These factors are not static; they continuously influence each other through a complex system of links that gives life and develops a community. The second step then, is to identify such links and examine how they strengthen a community and encourage progress or alternatively, contribute towards its decline. But first we must examine the factors themselves.

Goodness

The civic and historical thrust that runs through the whole Bible is aimed at driving humanity towards one common end, to be a holy people and citizens of a "holy city"[33]. There are two sides to this. On the one hand, it is issued as a command[34],

---

[31] See J. D. R. de Raadt, 2000, 2001; Veronica de Raadt, 2002; J. D. R. de Raadt and Veronica D. de Raadt, 2014.

[32] Each of these factors corresponds to a modality or aspect of God's Creation, see J. D. R. de Raadt, 2013, p. 90ff.

[33] Isaiah 52:1

[34] Leviticus 19:2; 20:26

as something to be performed: the people ought to be holy. On the other hand it is pronounced as a state or quality of God's people, regardless of any merit of their own. They are told that they *are* a holy nation[35]. The first points to the work at hand, the second is a title of ownership, a testament[36] to a future inheritance. That is why Paul addresses his people as "saints"[37], without requiring them to be canonised. This ought to encourage us to persevere in our civic endeavours. Anyone involved in social or institutional reform will know how hard it is to make progress and that the mere notion of change arouses a recalcitrant resistance in people. When these difficulties appear overwhelming, one is tempted to give up. Therefore, the assurance that the ultimate goal has been attained regardless of how many battles are lost is a great incentive to fight on.

But what does the Bible mean by the words *holy* and *saint*? The OT uses the words that are commonly translated into *holy*, *perfection* and *goodness* as synonyms of each other[38], removing any otherworldly meaning from it. It is a perfection of pure flesh and blood. For example, perfection is ascribed to animals that came from an ordinary herd or flock – bullocks, rams and lambs – and chosen as an offering[39]. It is also found in human crafts[40], in knowledge[41] and in speech[42]. Given that the words *holy* and *perfect* are often misinterpreted and understood as something that transcends the created order, we will refer to it simply as *goodness*. The Bible does not ascribe

---

[35] Deuteronomy 7:6; 14:2, 21; 1 Peter 2:9
[36] Ephesians 1:14
[37] For example Philippians 1:1
[38] Compare holy (*qadowch*, H6918) in Leviticus 11:44, perfect (*tamiyin*, H8549) in Genesis 17:1 and Deuteronomy 18:13 and good (*towb*, H2896) in Genesis 1:31.
[39] Exodus 29:1; Leviticus 22:21
[40] Exodus 35:31-35; in this passage the goodness of the work is implied in the remarkable skill with which God's Spirit has endowed the craftsman
[41] Job 36:4 (*tamiyin*, H8549)
[42] Amos 5:10; this passage refers to speech that is perfect by qualifying it with the term *tamiyin* (H8549).

goodness to just a limited set of things; its scope is wide open[43] and covers the whole from the light of day to marriage. The first chapter of Genesis ends with a general statement that everything God created was good, but it further hammers the fact by repeatedly referring to particular things as good – light, land, seas, grass, herbs and trees[44]. To be a perfect person therefore, is to assume the flesh and blood standards of Eden in everyday life and not to withdraw from it into a monastic existence.

Conversely, sin in the Bible is not just debauchery; its standards are far higher than this. The sin in the Bible[45] is "to miss a mark... [and a]... failure to live up to expectations"[46]. In other words, sin includes not only the extremes but the mediocrity that often passes unnoticed. Examples of God strongly reproving mediocrity abound[47], something that should shake up the complacency of societies where the mediocre far outnumber the debauchee. This applies especially because it is more likely for the debauchee to mend their way than for the second-rate person to straighten his[48].

But we must return to our theme of biblical goodness and compare it with the way Greek philosophy conceived it, especially Plato and Aristotle, both of whom would have great influence on Christian thought. Neither of these philosophers regarded the world as *created* out of nothing, as it were straight out of God's mind. They thought the world was *produced* by God placing an already pre-existent model upon it. Perfection was not to be found in whatever was produced,

---

[43] The root of the Hebrew word *towb* (H2896) '... refers to "good" or "goodness" in its broadest sense. Five general areas of meaning can be noted: 1) practical, economic or material good; 2) abstract goodness such as desirability, pleasantness and beauty; 3) quality or expense; 4) moral goodness and 5) technical philosophical good.' TWOT

[44] Genesis 1:10,12,18,21,25,31; 2:9,12,17,18

[45] In the OT the word is *chata'* (H2400), in the NT it is *hamartia* (G266).

[46] TWOT 638

[47] They are usually associated with weakness and lack of courage: Numbers 20:12 refers to Moses' weak leadership; Matthew 25:24-28 tells of a servant who failed to put his talent to work for fear of losing it.

[48] Matthew 21:31

but in the model that shaped it; a rose may be beautiful according to Plato, but never as perfectly beautiful as the model that produced it. The biblical position on this is exactly the opposite. It regards the rose as perfectly beautiful because it is the work of God's hands[49] without the intervention of any model. This is true about the rose and about everything else that God created, including man himself[50]. Granted, there are roses ruined by aphids and that are not beautiful at all and among men, who God has crowned with glory and honour, we find nasty characters such as Nero and Adolf Hitler. Yet despite the fall of man, the Creation still sufficiently displays some of its original goodness, so that God's demands upon us are not beyond the order that we can empirically observe around us.

Work

Work is an integral ingredient in the lives of both God and man. The living God reveals himself as a worker who acts through the mediation of his Spirit; likewise, he created man in order to work, first in his garden and then in other projects he had planned for him[51]. One must discern however two types of work; the first is the toil necessary to provide for our daily bread and survive[52]. It is a curse that follows the fall of man and which enslaved him. From this curse Christ freed him[53] so that he was now able to dedicate himself to a second type of work which, like God's own work, was creative and of service to him. The church has mistakenly identified this type of work with the worship of God. This is not so; Christ united the interests of God with those of humanity, so there could be no doubt that service to God meant service to humanity[54].

---

[49]   Psalm 111:7
[50]   Psalm 8:3-6
[51]   Genesis 2:15; Ephesians 2:10
[52]   Genesis 3:19
[53]   Matthew 6:33
[54]   Matthew 25:40

Worship became *workship*[55]. To distinguish both types of work, I will refer to the type of work that is meant merely to earn a living as *employment.* I will reserve the word *work* for that which has a social focus and addresses not our own individual needs but the needs of others. Specifically, it means rebuilding a community into a city of peace and excellence[56]. For God might be the ultimate builder[57], but we have to do the work. We were created for work and work is our destiny.

Moreover, God has undertaken to provide the sustenance for his labourers so that they may be able to engage themselves in this civic labour free from the encumbrance of "what we shall eat or what we shall drink?". In the OT, God not only freed Israel from slavery, but also released them from paid employment[58]. For he provided each family with their own land to sustain them and, in order to secure their ongoing freedom, forbade them to sell it[59]. Jesus promised the same sustenance to those who laboured for his kingdom.[60] On this basis, we may define true freedom as working for what one believes in, independently from one's source of sustenance. Conversely, bondage is having to work to sustain oneself, no matter how well paid. It is the purpose of our work that makes us free. The freeman lives for work, the slave works in order to live[61].

Nevertheless, work, that is developing a society to match God's plan, requires talent and skills which are provided by his Spirit. Therefore, in the OT the Spirit turned Bezaleel into a master of several crafts and, as we can gather from the account, he excelled in all of them. He contributed to the

---

[55] Workship would stand for the word *ergon* in the Greek NT, as used for example in Ephesians 2:10

[56] Isaiah 9:6, 58:12; Revelation 3:12, 21:2

[57] Hebrews 11:10

[58] Solomon, to his shame, reversed this

[59] Leviticus 25:23

[60] Matthew 6:33; Luke 12:31

[61] This principle applies as much today as it did in the ancient world and to rich countries as much as to poor ones. Most employees in rich countries may be affluent but, to gain their affluence, they have forfeited their freedom and sold themselves as a "human resource".

building of the tabernacle, where God was to reside among his people. But now that God resides among us, the people have become his tabernacle, his temple and his city[62]. Therefore, we require skills to build a community and, among the requisite skills, the social and pedagogical sciences play an important role. And the standard to be attained is extremely high, for every one of God's citizens must, in addition to being a free worker, be a nobleman[63].

We are not talking about an inherited nobility, a nobility of blood, but an inner nobility of the heart, mind and soul of every person. For Ortega y Gasset this nobility is:

> ... synonymous with a life of effort, ever set on excelling oneself, in passing beyond what one is to what one sets up as a duty and an obligation. In this way the noble life stands opposed to the common or inert life, which reclines statically upon itself, condemned to perpetual immobility, unless an external force compels it to come out of itself.[64]

Moreover, the talent required to build a noble community like this must spread to every one of its members[65]. Therefore, the Spirit is given to everyone[66], not just a few, endowing every citizen with the power to fulfil his vocation wherever he has been called to serve with excellence, doing wonderful works[67].

This brings us to a subject which is much misunderstood but which we must consider due to its close relationship with work. I refer to miracles. The English word miracle – and the equivalent in other European languages – is rooted in the Latin word *miraculum*. It is a word with many imputed meanings that are not necessarily biblical. It is often inserted in English translations of the Bible even though it is clearly absent in the

---

[62] 1 Corinthians 3:16, 6:19; Ephesians 2:19-22, Revelation 21:10
[63] 1 Peter 2:5,9
[64] Ortega y Gasset, 1996, VII
[65] Kuyper 2000, 1, 2, VIII, dedicates a whole chapter to the wide breadth of gifts and talents that are given by the Spirit.
[66] Joel 2:28-29
[67] Romans 12:6-8

original text. The misunderstanding is partly caused by making a distinction between natural and supernatural phenomena and partly because miracles have been taken out of the historical context within which they took place. The Greek idea of nature is largely the culprit behind this, an idea that has enslaved European man, according to Ortega y Gasset[68]. It has also enslaved Christianity.

Nature, Aristotle taught us, was governed by a cause-and-effect chain linked together by a logic that allowed a person to predict an effect once its cause was identified. Aristotle believed God's involvement with the world was limited to being the "prime mover", that is, providing the first cause and thereafter removing himself from any further interference. Since the world was not perfect and God's interest was limited to perfection, he withdrew from it after the first cause to contemplate his own perfection. Now, from its very beginning, Christian theology has accommodated itself to this idea of nature and added to it a super-nature where it could conveniently place miracles safely beyond the critical reach of Greek logic. However, by doing this, it limited the scope of God's sovereignty over his Creation and turned the miracles into some kind of magic.

But the Bible admits no such division between natural and supernatural realms; it does not even acknowledge that nature is independent and ruled exclusively by cause-and-effect laws. It insists that all effects – including their presumed causes – happen by the direct intervention of God's Spirit and they happen at his total discretion. It is the Spirit who is the ultimate worker in the world, the person who keeps all things going. If an event regularly appears to follow causes, it is only because the Spirit orders it that way according to his own pleasure and to reveal to us how we should respond to these actions. His revelation is pivotal, for this order is far more complex than the simplistic conceptions of Aristotle.

Furthermore, miracles are often taken out of their historical context, especially the manner in which they are mapped from

---

[68] 2004

the NT onto the OT historical record. The central contact point between the two testaments is the release of the Hebrew slaves from their Egyptian oppressors and the coming of Christ – the promised Messiah – in order to release all peoples from sin. To the first was promised a land of milk and honey, to the latter the city of God. Thus, Moses and Christ's roles correspond to each other, both are deliverers of oppressed people. Now, miracles in the Bible heavily congregate around these two emancipatory events as their symbolic markers. There are several words in the original documents used to identify these markers[69]. Their objective is to show visually to people the power of God that is being applied to liberate them[70] from their oppressors and to organise them into a nation. The exercise of this power is not a one-sided matter; it involves both God on the one side and his people on the other. God fought for the Israelites to conquer Canaan[71], but it was their blood that was spilled on the battleground. Likewise, in the NT, the power of God's Spirit that redeemed his people by raising Christ from the dead also invests the people with the intellectual power – rather than physical – to fight for their territory[72].

This intellectual power includes revelation, knowledge and wisdom[73]. All knowledge starts with revelation. Often we think that revelation means disclosing things that transcend the world in which we live. In fact, those who, like Paul, have been given a glimpse of what lies beyond this world are barred from speaking about it[74]. What revelation is really about is the order by which the Spirit regulates the events in this world and which were a mystery before they were revealed. The gradual removal of such mysteries has led to the wonderful works we have been able to carry out; attainments which Christ himself

---

[69] These are the Hebrew words *mophets* (H4159) and *owth* (H226) in the OT and the Greek *semeion* (G4592) used in the NT.
[70] Exodus 9:13-16
[71] Joshua 23:10
[72] 2 Corinthians 10:4-5
[73] Ephesians 1:17-21
[74] 2 Corinthians 122-4

foresaw and which he claimed would surpass his own works[75]. Jesus cured a limited number of people of their diseases, but the wonders of modern medicine surpass this when it entirely eradicates some diseases such as polio or when it dramatically reduces infant mortality or the death of mothers through childbirth. To these must be added our amazing technology, urban hygiene, the comforts of our homes and many other advances. It is irreverent and ungrateful not to acknowledge that all the marvels of science and technology that we enjoy today are gifts of the Spirit – and not to consider them as the milk and honey that Christ promised us. It is sheer madness and unforgivable ignorance that in the midst of these wonders of modern times, secularism should go unchallenged and even be embraced by so many scholars.

But work, whether marvellous or ordinary, requires vision, education and organisation; we turn to examine these in the next chapter.

---

[75]   John 14:12

3 Community, Education and Vision

Social Organisation

To be effective in developing their communities, people need to organise and manage their work[76]. This is a vast topic but here we will briefly discuss only two variables of social organisation: the size of the social unit and its leadership. The proper structure of any social unit ought to be very much determined by its need to disseminate information and knowledge among its members. In turn, the amount of information and knowledge required and the place within the organisation where it should be channelled depends both on the objectives of the organisation and the environmental challenges it faces when attaining them[77]. In this, one must strike a balance between social autonomy on the one hand, and centralisation on the other. Smaller social units with a high degree of information and knowledge and the independence to put them into effect tend to respond more rapidly and effectively to environmental changes than larger and more centralised social groups. The advantage of a decentralised organisational structure can be observed not only in human societies but also in natural systems. Much of our body organs and the nervous system that transmits information to them are highly decentralised; thus, a person does not need to tell his heart when and at what rate to beat. The same principle of decentralisation can be observed in all living systems be they vegetable, animal or human. It can also be observed in the patriarchal family unit in the Bible and in other contemporary communities[78]; they are economically self-sustainable and highly independent. Some may regard this sort of organisation as primitive, but this is not true. It is a structure that responded to all of life, including essential human needs which have not changed at all with time.

---

[76]   1 Corinthians 4:1; 1 Peter 4:10; the word for manager is *oikonomos* (G3623), the root of the modern word *economist*.
[77]   J. D. R. de Raadt, 2015
[78]   The Hebrew and Greek words for this family unit or household is respectively *bayith* (H1004) and *oikos* (G3624).

There are however, other objectives that entail work of a greater magnitude (one cannot build a large ship in one's garage). This work can only be carried out by incorporating smaller groups into a larger social organisation. In ancient society, this larger group was the tribe, which now would correspond to a small municipality. To function effectively, these larger groups must centralise some of the control of the operations, thus proportionally removing flexibility and freedom from the smaller units that comprise it. It is important that a fine balance between centralisation and decentralisation be reached so that the overall benefits gained by the complete set of social units outweigh the disadvantages[79]. Moreover, centralisation should only be deployed while it is needed; it should not be allowed to perpetuate itself. Centralisation is similar to a medical drug; too much of it, for too long a time, turns it into poison. When the degree of centralisation exceeds the required level – which is what happens in bureaucracies – it hinders, rather than enhances, the capability of the organisation to attain its objectives. Why would this be allowed? Centralisation means accumulation of power by an individual or a small number of people and power tends to corrupt. Often it is also true that the corrupt seek such power.

A biblical illustration of this follows Israel's exit from Egypt and its settling in Canaan. Such a major operation required the centralised leadership of Moses, and later Joshua, at a national[80] rather than tribal level. Once the people were established in the promised land, centralised leadership at the national level ended and a greater degree of autonomy and localised leadership arose at the tribal level. Yet, each time Israel was threatened by its neighbours, control was once more cent-

---

[79] Socio-cybernetics is one science that aims at establishing the precise optimum combination of centralisation and decentralisation in social organisations, e.g. Beer, 1994 and J. D. R. de Raadt, 2015.

[80] I use the term *national* not in the modern sense, but in the restricted sense of Israel as a people united by a common ethnic origin and purpose and assembled into twelve tribes.

ralised and a judge[81] from one of the tribes assumed leadership at a national level. This was for a military purpose only and when the threat was removed, leadership reverted to the tribal level. When Samuel, the last of the judges, became old, the people requested a different type of leadership. They desired to have a permanent king set over them who would establish an Israelite dynasty. I quote at length what God thought of this foolish idea:

> ...This will be the manner of the king that shall reign over you: he will take your sons, and appoint them unto him, for his chariots, and to be his horsemen; and they shall run before his chariots: and he will appoint them unto him for captains of thousands and captains of fifties; and he will set some to plough his ground, and to reap his harvest, and to make his instruments of war, and the instruments of his chariots. And he will take your daughters to be confectioneries, and to be cooks, and to be bakers. And he will take your fields, and your vineyards, and your olive yards, even the best of them, and give them to his servants. And he will take the tenth of your seed, and of your vineyards, and give to his officers, and to his servants. And he will take your menservants, and your maidservants, and your goodliest young men, and your asses, and put them to his work. He will take the tenth of your flocks: and you shall be his servants.[82]

How true these words were! Solomon was Israel's greatest exploiter. Despite his wisdom, he fell prey to extravagant ambition. He built large buildings and other such projects, along with a bureaucracy to control them, in order to aggrandise himself. It certainly did not improve the lot of his people. On the contrary, they were eventually forced to sell the land that

---

[81] The word *judge* used to translate the original Hebrew word *shaphat* (H8199) does not convey an accurate idea. The Spanish c*audillo* would be closer to the original meaning.

[82] 1 Samuel 8:11-17

sustained them and become his employees. They ended up being of a status that was not much better than they had under Pharaoh in Egypt[83]. This has repeated itself over and over again in history and not only with monarchs, but also with so-called democratically elected leaders. They did not serve the people, but used the people to serve them.

Education

We have argued that a community that is free, autonomous and at its best serves the human needs of its members and must evenly distribute information and knowledge among them. That is, it must be an educated community as it was envisaged six centuries before the birth of Christ by the prophet Jeremiah[84]. Christ sought to fulfil Jeremiah's prophecy by making education the spearhead of his mission and by turning every citizen into a student[85]. The truth, he said, will make people free[86] and this makes sense not only at the individual but also at the organisational and social level. It also has immediate bearing on the type of leadership that a community needs. Therefore Paul wisely required, apart from character, one main skill from leaders, that is, an ability to teach[87]. This is sound sociological thinking; if one wants a community that is small and autonomous, then its members must be well educated. A leader who is a skilled teacher will ensure this, especially when he endeavours to reproduce his own skills by teaching others how to teach[88]. In this light, one can sympathise with Paul's frustration – and that of the author of Hebrews

---

[83] 1 Kings 5:13-16, 9:15-22
[84] Jeremiah 31:33-34
[85] The word disciple is the translation of the Greek *mathetes* (G3101) in the original, which means a pupil or learner, MLSJ
[86] John 8:32
[87] 1 Timothy 3:2
[88] 2 Timothy 2:2

– with people who did not wish to think and were content with intellectual milk[89].

History and Vision

As I have stated before, I prefer to use the word *vision* rather than *faith*, for it more accurately renders the meaning behind the Biblical idea[90]. Vision is so close to history that it is impossible to understand one without the other, thus we shall – with the assistance of Figure 3-1 – examine these two factors together. In this figure history appears divided into three sections separated first by the fall of man and then by our death or the return of Christ. Since it is more likely that our death will occur first, we will focus our attention on death. We have labelled these sections as *Eden, our time* and the *hereafter*. Life after death is important, because a life ought to be a reflection of what takes place after death (arrow 1). This is not a pessimistic view of things; on the contrary, a creative and historical life constantly pulls the hereafter onto this side of time (as the direction of arrow 1 suggests). Life without it is vacuous. In a letter to an atheist friend of his, Unamuno wrote:

> I do not say that we deserve a hereafter, nor that logic demonstrates it; I say that I needed it – whether I deserved it or not – and nothing else. I say that what now happens does not satisfy me, that I thirst for eternity. I need that, I n-e-e-d it! And without that there is no joy in living or the joy of living means nothing. It is very easy to say: "one must live, one must content oneself with life!" What about us who are not content with it? .... I do not sacrifice my pleasures and my present needs, my greatest need at present it to think about the hereafter.[91]

---

[89] 1 Corinthians 3:2-3; the author of Hebrews (5:12-13) also reveals a level of frustration.
[90] See J. D. R. de Raadt, 2013, p. 59
[91] Robles, 1996, p. 141

How can we think of the hereafter if we are not permitted to see it[92]? Although we may not be able to see it, we do have sufficient information to build a vision of it that inspires and motivates our work in this life. If we know that after our death we shall once more be in Eden[93], we must look back to Eden in Genesis and the historical events thereafter from which to draw our vision.

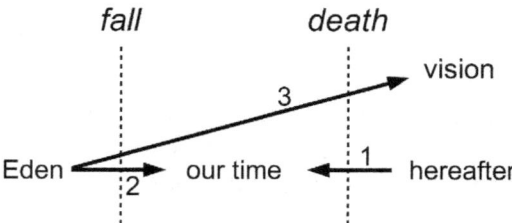

Figure 3-1: History and Vision

The fall of Adam did not completely obliterate the goodness of God's Creation nor the cultural command he issued to him and Eve to work and develop his Creation. There is still before us the beauty and majesty of the natural world to admire – mountains, rivers, the sea, trees and flowers, birds, animals and so on (arrow 2). But we can also savour the cultural work of man – beautiful buildings, scientific and technological advances; the fine arts with their music, paintings, sculpture and literature are also part of the Creation of God, delivered by artists, craftsmen and scientists inspired by the Holy Spirit. They realised the work that God had planned beforehand for

---

[92] One exception is Paul, who was permitted to see it (2 Corinthians 12:4) but forbidden to say what he saw. This sounds reasonable. Having a glimpse of the hereafter, resembling the world in which we now live with all its wonders and beauty, but without dishonest politicians and their lies, without bureaucracy, without the oppressive intrusion of the media and commercial propaganda, without disease and the infirmities of age, makes it harder, I imagine, to face our times. It would hinder our work.

[93] Luke 23:43

them to do[94]. And all these wonders, both natural and cultural, standing right before our eyes, in our present times, are interlinked parts of a systemic totality which the Bible sometimes calls paradise, God's Kingdom, God's city or by some other name. Yet regardless of the name given, it is what true Christianity is supposed to be, an overarching vision of the hereafter, a birds-eye view that, although it transcends death, is yet based on a concrete and historical reality. Eden, therefore is not only present now but also is the model of the vision that inspires us to work (arrow 3). This concreteness is confirmed by the all-encompassing reconciliation that Christ has brought upon everything[95]. Unamuno beautifully affirms it to his atheist friend:

> Every day my faith assumes a more concrete and his-torical character and I remove myself from vagaries. I am re-establishing in my conscience a personal and evangelical God, the father of Christ...There is no health for modern people outside Christianity.[96]

Unamuno was right then (he wrote this in 1902) and he is right now. Apart from Christianity, there is no other perspective of life that can pull us out of our predicament. This is not a matter of dogma, it is a matter of recovering our humanity in the midst of the social muddle of modernity. Yet this muddle ought not to blind us, for we have been given God's Spirit to sift the good from the bad[97] and to learn the competence necessary to perform the work that has been appointed for us. And as we learn, we and our work are purified, just as minerals are purified by fire which separates the slag from the clean metal[98]. At our death we will find that the produce of our labour, completely purified, will perfectly

---

[94] Ephesians 2:10
[95] Colossians 1:19-20
[96] Robles, 1996, p.135
[97] Philippians 4:8-9
[98] 1 Corinthians 3:13; Philippians 1:6, 1 Peter 1:7

fit into God's full design, just as a piece fits into a jigsaw puzzle. This will follow immediately after our death; Christ's reply to the outlaw crucified by his side was that he would enter into Eden *that day*[99]. The Greek word in the original[100] stresses the immediacy of that event, there is no waiting in purgatory, nor entering into dormancy nor even waiting for Christ's second coming. It would happen that day. For when we die we step out of the time zone of this world to another where a thousand years here is but one day over there[101]. That is why, as some have said, every person carries within himself the history of all humanity, its beginning as well as its end. Though we cannot explain this, it emphasises the importance of each life and the work that has been assigned to it.

The Community Model

The description above of the factors will have already sug-gested how closely linked they are with each other. These links are a manifestation of a dynamic[102] that drives history and where the impact of each factor shapes the other. I have built a socio-cultural model showing a selection of links between factors and their links – see Figure 3-2. Each circle represents a factor and the arrows stand for their links. Potentially there are 28 such arrows, but I have limited our scope to only eight which I regard as the most strategically relevant[103]. They can drive the community towards life and development and away from decline and death.

---

[99] Luke 23:43; the Greek word *paradeisos* (G3857) means a park which the NT uses to refer to Eden.
[100] *Semeron* (G4594), can mean today, now or at present.
[101] Psalm 90:4; 2 Peter 3:8
[102] Greek *dunamis* (G1411), see Acts 1:8
[103] I have based this selection on our empirical research in diverse com-munities in Europe and Australia.

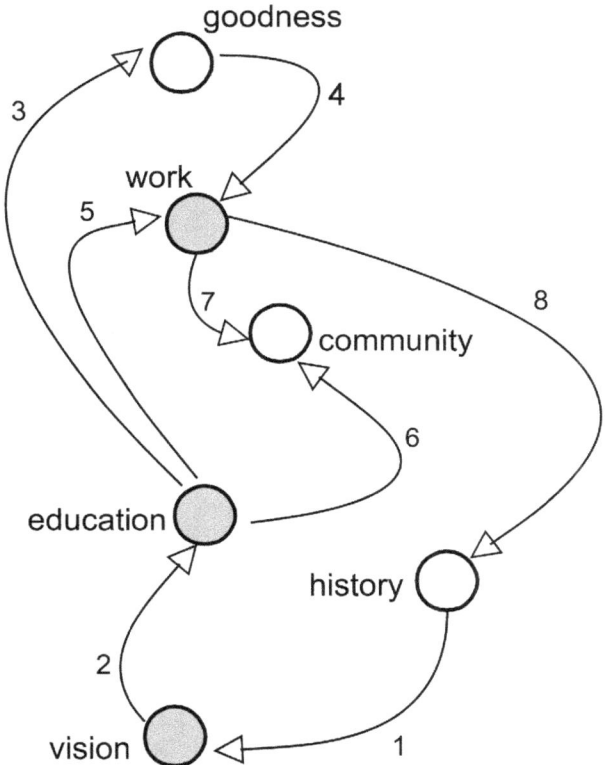

Figure 3-2: The Community Model

The figure highlights in grey the three factors – vision, education and work – that play a central role in transforming a vision into reality. Here is where the action that changes history takes place. Let us examine each of these arrows in detail. We have already discussed the link between history and vision (arrow 1) and need no further elaboration at this stage. Arrow 2 singles out vision as the necessary foundation of a good education; education ought to begin with a solid grasp of the historical significance, for all humanity, of the emancipation of Israel from the bondage of Egypt and the liberation by Christ from the bondage of sin (arrow 1). We used to teach it to little children, for everything else that the Bible teaches runs along the historical path marked by these two momentous events. This covers about everything, from justice to family life to agriculture. I do not mean to say that the Bible's coverage of these matters is exhaustive or even sufficient to live, but it contains a small fragment of almost every field of knowledge that an educated person should master. Here we are mostly interested in three fields of knowledge – goodness, work and social organisation. We need not cite Biblical references about teaching goodness (arrow 3) to young and old, they are everywhere. But it is of no use to speak of goodness – or love for that matter – unless it is put into practice; therefore the word good is repeatedly accompanied by work, especially in the NT[104], an association which is represented by arrow 4.

Performing good works in order to fulfil people's needs in turn requires competence, therefore the necessary working skills should also be taught[105] (arrow 5). This combination of arrows 2 and 5 distinguishes vocational work from employment; that is, performing work in which one believes because it is part of one's vision as well as because one is competent to carry it out.

What is often ignored nowadays is that we must also teach people to organise themselves (arrow 6). For "Jesus also organised"[106] as did the law given to Israel in the OT that set up social structures for families, tribes, leadership and economy. Paul was a great organiser, as we have already seen regarding leadership; the subject often recurs in his epistles. If

---

[104] E.g. Matthew 5:16; Ephesians 2:10; Titus 2:14
[105] Exodus 18:20; 2 Timothy 3:16-17; Titus 2:7; Titus 3:14
[106] Kuyper, 1950, p. 30; emphasis in the original

we do not teach people to organise themselves, especially the young, someone else will organise them to serve the interests of the rich and powerful. It is imperative therefore that we teach people to organise themselves so that their work serves both the immediate and long-term needs of the community (arrow 7) and not the vested interests of privileged groups. The motto "organise or perish" is applicable here. Only by doing this will we be able to change the path of history and labour for God's city, represented by arrow 8. This arrow closes a loop formed by the arrows that run through its perimeter (1, 2, 3, 4 and 8). The loop has a multiplying effect; it aims to develop a community, making it better – that is, more just, more beautiful and more ethical – through each one of its cycles. In addition, it has a transferable effect toward other communities, encouraging them to emulate the patterns of the first. This loop, no matter how poorly represented by our operationalisation, stands for the leaven[107] of God's city; it is the power which God's Spirit released upon the early disciples to change the world. In a space of about seventy years, out of a small group in Jerusalem, similarly patterned communities appeared in various places of the Roman Empire energised by the same loop.

Transition from Hebrew to Hellenic Culture

The Hebrews were an earthy people. They were expected to love life on earth because it was God's Creation and a gift to them. They were expected to love their wine, their food, their parties and all other blessings which they believed had come from the hand of God. They were to love family life, have a large brood of children and be thoroughly social and not at all individualists. The Hebrews were not pantheists, but the relationship between God and them was firmly grounded on the concreteness of his Creation. God's residence in their midst

---

[107] Matthew 13:33

was in the ark of the covenant, where the tablets of the law were deposited. This law was a down-to-earth law, it regulated their food, their health, their families and all other things concerned with life here on earth. God was not an impersonal deity but a father to them, he was above definitions or even naming. He was the one he was, full stop[108]. Although it may sound odd at first, this sentence makes perfect sense. It emphasises the factualness of God, he must be fully received as he presents himself and in no other way. We often say more or less the same when people set expectations over us which do not correspond to ourselves. We say: we are who we are.

The incarnation of Jesus the Messiah was a reaffirmation of all of this, God's people could now relate to him as a man rather than as some transcendental divinity. His disciples shared Christ's life, they travelled with him as friends and experienced all the adventures that a journey brings. Jesus must have often arrived as tired and hungry as them at their destination, perhaps sometimes they found no available accommodation and had to sleep in the open air or – again! – in some barn among the cattle. They also partook together of community life in wedding parties and other invitations to dinner and in the everyday social encounter in markets. Good wine was an important ingredient to the joy of celebrations and Jesus, at least once, ensured that they should not run out of it. He was Emmanuel, God among men and women, he was one of them; despite his status and mission, he requested no privileges but to share in their life as another human being. Therefore, his disciples believed in him as one believes in a friend. Since Jesus' disciples became the leaders of the church, they too imprinted their Hebraic world-view on the communities they founded. They taught that man lived in God's Creation, that they had a cultural mandate to fill the earth and a Gospel to fight for a city of which God himself was the builder. It is this

---

[108] Exodus 3:14

earthy world-view which we have tried to operationalise in the last chapter.

But momentous events in the first century meant that this picture was to change radically from the beginning of the second century. Firstly, the church was violently persecuted in Jerusalem following the death of Stephen and dispersed as far as Phoenicia and Cyprus. Yet, it formed a rather solid Christian community in Antioch, which became the base for the missionary journeys of Paul and his colleagues. Therefore, the geographical centre of church expansion shifted from Jewish to gentile territory and from then on the largest number of converts came from a gentile, rather than a Jewish background. As may have been expected, when the apostles died, their successors to the leadership – known as the Early Church Fathers or just Church Fathers – were mostly non-Jews.

The second event was the destruction of Jerusalem in 70AD. At this point in time, Judea, the historical remnant of ancient Israel, ceased to exist as a nation. The Jews lost their territory and became aliens for the next two millenniums. It led to the final separation of Christianity from Judaism, partly because Christians did not join the Jews in the defence of Jerusalem. It also removed from the Mediterranean world the concrete reality of the people of the OT as a nation with its own political system, its capital city and the temple that stood on it. To the eyes of the world, Judaism was now just another religion rather than the nation – with its own Hebraic culture and roots about two thousand years old – that originated when Joshua led the invasion of Canaan. Something similar happened to Christianity. Like a ship, it sailed out of its Jewish moorings into a Hellenic sea of culture and began to blend itself with a social organisation and religious philosophy that gradually transformed it, like Judaism, from a civic movement into a religious system.

The change began almost immediately after the death of the Jewish apostles when the leadership passed on to Hellenic

Christians. Hellenism covered a vast territory and with it, diverse strands, but for the purpose of our study we are only interested in two main elements deeply grounded in its world view: its philosophy and its social organisation. We discussed Greek philosophy earlier[109] but we will briefly mention its main features again. To begin with, its intellectual focus was not empirical reality, but the world of ideas and abstracts. Particularly in the period which we are dealing with (100 to 410 AD), this thinking had become so abstract that it had turned into a mystical blend of philosophy with religion[110]. And yet despite this mysticism, its thinking and reasoning still claimed to be based on logic, regardless of how unintelligible and entangled that logic might be. Moreover, the static nature of earlier Greek philosophy was also preserved. Since the world was eternal, truth was as immobile as a geometrical theorem resulting in a way of thinking and believing that had no conception of history.

In addition to this Hellenic culture, Christians had also to contend with the Roman emperors, who saw Christ as threatening their claims to divinity. From its very first days, Christianity had to face opposition, first by the Pharisees and priests who persecuted Jesus, and then by Judaism which, in general, opposed the apostles. To its list of antagonists was now added Caesar. Yet, there was an important difference in the way that Jesus and the apostles fought back when compared to the Church Fathers. Jesus and the apostles defended themselves with historical facts; the apostles were adamant that the death and resurrection of Christ was a witnessed event. But the Church Fathers changed their mode of attack, they sought to transpose the Gospel into the Hellenic framework of philosophy and to defend Christianity on that ground. Here they committed a fatal blunder. They were like a team of soccer players agreeing to play their game on a cricket pitch hit-

---

[109] J. D. R. de Raadt, 2013
[110] Tillich, 1968

ting the ball with a bat instead of their feet. They were bound to lose their fight right from the start. They may have not capitulated nor adopted their opponents' ideas, but they certainly adopted their epistemology – that is, the way of thinking by which these ideas were reached.

And, in addition to surrendering the historical ground of reasoning, the Church Fathers deserted the Holy Spirit as well. According to Paul Tillich:

> One can say that in the generation of the...[Early Church]... Fathers, the great visions of the first ecstatic breakthrough had disappeared, and that instead of that, a given set of ideas was left, a set of ideas which produced a kind of ecclesiastical conformity and made the missionary work possible. Some people have complained about this development, complained that so early after the second generation the power of the Spirit was on the wane. But this is an unavoidable thing in all creative periods. After the breakthrough – one only needs to think of the Reformation – and after the first generation which received the breakthrough (i.e., the second generation), a fixation or concentration on some special points begins; the need to preserve what was given, the educational needs – all this working together to a Christianity which, compared with the Christianity of the Apostolic age, had considerably lost its Spiritual power.[111]

One can understand how people in the 2nd century, nurtured in a Hellenic culture, could have made such a mistake. What is difficult to understand is that right up to our present times, except for a short period during the Christian Renascence, theologians were to repeat this blunder, something any sufficiently shrewd scientist would avoid. Even Tillich, by no means a conservative theologian, fell into the trap[112].

---

[111] 1968, p. 17
[112] Tillich was an existentialist theologian.

Almost as soon as the Church Fathers took over leadership from the apostles, this "ecclesiastical conformity" sustained a transformation of the church from a community into what Tillich called an "institution for salvation"[113], but which may be more appropriately labelled a bureaucracy for salvation. The process was fully complete by the time of Cyprian, that is, by the middle of the third century. What followed from then on was simply a consolidation of this bureaucracy, highlighted by the emperor Constantine becoming a Christian. He provided the church with basilicas for worship and called for church councils to establish religious orthodoxy.

A community is the natural habitat of humans. People need to belong to a community to grow physically and culturally; it is as necessary as water is for fish. However, it is a need not often recognised today. Only in a community can a person actively integrate every aspect of his life into the social dimension. The local baker may also be a father, an uncle and a cousin. If he is a typically active community member, he may also play as goalkeeper in the local football team, sing with the community choir, volunteer in the fire-brigade and so on. Women are even more community-minded and are normally seen to be active everywhere. Community integration and active participation are the marks of a good citizen and also a requisite for a healthy and well rounded cultural life. The Bible conceives God's people always as a community, never as a bureaucracy. The Hebrews were released from Egypt in order to be a community and obedience to the Law – which included every realm of life – ensured it. Nothing would have been further from Jesus' mind to reject this OT precedent and to re-organise his church as a bureaucracy. The apostles must have understood this when they, from the very beginning, organised themselves into a community that shared its belongings[114].

---

[113] Tillich, 1968, p. 101
[114] Acts 2:44-45

Weber was probably the first to identify the church as a bureaucracy. He identified three properties that are of interest to us: (1) it serves "ideal or material ends"[115], (2) it possesses specialised knowledge and (3) it controls its operations on the basis of this knowledge.[116] We can recognise each of these elements in the church, where with time, service chiefly signified worship – including the sacraments – knowledge turned into orthodoxy and its instrument of control was theology in the hands of the clergy led by bishops or some similar higher office. Therefore, bureaucratisation changed three of the factors we defined in Figure 3-2: work, vision and community became respectively worship, orthodoxy[117] and bureaucracy. The other factors changed as well and I have listed this transformation in Table 3-1 along with the names of the Early Fathers who most contributed to it. Their names are listed in the left-hand column with the approximate dates of their birth and death. I have omitted history from the factors, for they did not show much interest or understanding of it[118], at least not in the biblical sense. At the top of the table I have listed the original factors in Figure 3-2 and at the bottom what they became by the time Cyprian died. In between them and next to the name of each Early Father, I have shown with a down arrow (♦) how he contributed to this transformation. The exception in this was Clement of Alexandria, for what he wrote is in far greater accordance with the original factors than with the transformed ones. We may say that he swam against the cur-

---

[115] Weber, 2009. Weber was a German sociologist best known for his work on bureaucracy and the relationship between Protestantism and economics.

[116] When specialisation and control are pushed to their extreme, they create an assembly line type of organisation.

[117] Orthodoxy (*orthodoxia*) is a Greek word; its literal meaning is "right opinion" (LSJ) but among Christians it became a synonym of the "right doctrine" or "the truth".

[118] The exceptions were Eusebius and Augustine, but they came at a later date.

rent of the other Fathers and, therefore, I have marked his contribution with an up arrow (↑).

Table 3-1 Transformation of the Factors

Early Fathers	Socio-Cultural Factors				
	GOODNESS	WORK	COMMUNITY	EDUCATION	VISION
Ignatius ?-107	↓		↓		↓
Justin 100-165		↓			↓
Irenaeus 125-202			↓	↓	↓
Tertullian 155-240	↓	↓	↓	↓	↓
Clement 150-215	↑	↑	↑	↑	↑
Origen 185-254	↓	↓		↓	↓
Cyprian 200-258)		↓	↓		
	ASCETICISM	WORSHIP	BUREAUCRACY	INDOCTRINATION	ORTHODOXY

This transformation took approximately one and half centuries to be completed – the period extended from Ignatius' letters to Cyprian's death – and in the next chapters we will examine the contribution of each of these Early Fathers to it. However, I must point out a limitation to our analysis. Our task is to examine the development of the church from a sociological and historical perspective and not a theological one. Unfortunately, the history of the church has been documented and written mainly by theologians and their interest has naturally been theological. This means that while we have documentary sources to trace the transformation of these socio-cultural factors in the minds of the Early Fathers, we have limited sociological data to determine at what time Christians adopted such transformations in practice. However, we do know they were eventually adopted, and that satisfactorily meets the requirements for our enquiry.

4 Ignatius

One of the first contributors towards the bureaucratisation of the church was Ignatius. His letters[119] were written around the end of the first century and beginning of the next while in transit to Rome to face trial. In them we find the first traces of orthodoxy, institutionalisation and asceticism that were to transform the church from a community into a bureaucracy.

Old Testament Undervalued

By orthodoxy I mean the fixed statements of faith, elaborated by theologians, which the church eventually adopted as mandatory and to which its members were to give assent[120]. We will see that the content of the orthodoxy was gradually built over time by abstracting select material from the NT and fitting it into a Hellenic rather than an OT mould. Ignatius' attitude towards the OT may have contributed to this; in his letter to the church in Philadelphia he wrote the following:

> The priests indeed are good, but the High Priest is better; to whom the holy of holies has been committed, and who alone has been trusted with the secrets of God. He is the door of the Father, by which enter in Abraham, and Isaac, and Jacob, and the prophets, and the apostles, and the Church. All these have for their object the attaining to the unity of God. But the Gospel possesses something transcendent [above the former dispensation], viz., the appearance of our Lord Jesus Christ, His passion and resurrection. For the beloved

---

[119] The authenticity of these letters has been a subject of much dispute. Some have claimed that several of them do not come from the hand of Ignatius – who died in the year 107 – but were written by someone else as late as the middle of the 3rd century. I have limited my references to the seven letters generally accepted as authentic (see Rius-Camps, 1977; Brent, 2007).

[120] A few centuries later, it gave rise to rigid creeds, such as the Athanasian that begins with the words "Whosoever will be saved: before all things it is necessary that he hold the Catholic Faith..." (Kerr, 1966).

prophets announced Him, but the Gospel is the perfection of immortality.[121]

This somewhat departed from the teaching position of Christ, who saw himself as a fulfiller of the OT[122] which meant that the events and ideas that were presented in the NT could only be rightly understood by connecting them to the OT. There was in addition, an important linguistic function of the OT when reading the NT. The latter was written in Koiné Greek, the common language spoken all over the Hellenic world and an excellent medium to disseminate the Gospel throughout the Mediterranean. However, there was a downside to this; like every language, it was very close to the way of thinking of the people who spoke it. Thought acts as a constraint on language and vice-versa. This was natural, for a language, as a means of communication, must have had words that were defined in a manner that related to the thoughts of the people who spoke it. But this meant that a person found it difficult to express his thoughts in a foreign language; and Hebrew and Hellenic people thought very differently.

One difference between these two ways of thinking was that Hellenic thought tended towards the conceptual and abstract while Hebrew focused on the concrete. These differences had an impact on their respective languages and how words and expressions should be interpreted. For example, in the Greek language the word for *world* was *kosmos* (G2889), which literally meant "orderly arrangement", "good order" or "form"[123]. These were rather foreign concepts for the Hebrew so when the NT made use of the word *kosmos* it generally meant two different things. When it is said that God loved the world[124], it means that he loved his Creation comprised by the earth and the sky[125]. On the other hand when it says that we should not

---

[121] Schaff, n.d.a., Epistle to the Philadelphians, IX

[122] It should be noted that Jesus categorically endorsed the authority of the OT, Matthew 5:17-18.

[123] MLSJ

[124] John 3:16

love the world[126], it means that we should not conform to patterns of living that were contrary to the Torah and that were not good for humanity. In the first instance, the word was used with a Hebrew idea in mind while in the second, it was meant in its Greek sense. Thus, a passage that at first appeared contradictory when words were interpreted according to the Greek lexicon, made sense once they were interpreted by referring to the OT. We will see how important it is to have the OT as an arbiter for the interpretation of the NT Koiné Greek and how foreign and damaging ideas can be drawn into Christian thought if the OT is either neglected or not properly understood.

Episcopal Control

Bureaucracies are controlled from the top down and, towards this objective, Ignatius' contribution is plain. He set the titles of bishop and presbyter – which in the NT are used interchangeably – into a rigidly centralised structure with the bishop at the top, presbyters next then followed by deacons. Authority ran rigidly from top to bottom and ultimately rested fully on the bishop:

> And do ye also reverence your bishop as Christ Himself, according as the blessed apostles have enjoined you. He that is within the altar is pure, wherefore also he is obedient to the bishop and presbyters: but he that is without is one that does anything apart from the bishop, the presbyters, and the deacons. Such a person is defiled in his conscience, and is worse than an infidel.[127]

This authority did not limit itself to matters that pertained to the church as a community, but appeared to extend itself to

---

[125] The Hebrew words for earth is *Tebel* (H8398) and *'erets* (H776) and *shamayim* (H8064) for sky.
[126] 1 John 2:15
[127] Schaff, n.d.a., Epistle to the Trallians, VII

every department of people's lives (including the decision to marry):

> As therefore the Lord did nothing without the Father, being united to Him, neither by Himself nor by the apostles, so neither do ye anything without the bishop and presbyters.[128]

This was the foundation of the episcopal system that was rapidly adopted everywhere but also the beginning of the separation of the people into two layers – clergy and laity. No such division was suggested in the NT. Paul's letters address a variety of men and women as fellow workers. No doubt Paul was a group leader, but there is no allusion to hierarchy – not even to bishop or presbyter – just "fellow workers"[129]. This is good organisational skill. One does a similar thing with dog sledding; a lead dog – the crucial group leader –is tied at the front and is followed by the other dogs. For the sled to travel smoothly, all dogs must run in the same direction and at the same speed. But the division between clergy – who regard themselves as ministers or servants – and laity resembles a sled race with the lead dog pulling by itself while the rest of the dogs ride on it. It is hardly surprising that the system does not work!

The Body and the Soul

Asceticism is defined as "the doctrine that through renunciation of worldly pleasures it is possible to achieve a high spiritual or intellectual state"[130]. Since most worldly pleasures are experienced through the body, it is the body that gets the brunt

---

[128] Schaff, n.d.a., Epistle to the Magnesians, VII; e.g. people needed the approval of the bishop to marry, Epistle to Polycarp, V; and if they did things without his approval they were regarded as lacking good conscience, Epistle to the Magnesians, IV.

[129] That is, *sunergos* (G4904) in the original; see Romans 16:9 & 21; 1 Corinthians 3:9; 2 Corinthians 8:23; Philippians 2:25, 4:3; Colossians 4:11; 1 Thessalonians 3:2; Philemon 1:1, 24

[130] Artha Dictionary, 2012

of deprivation, which is the substance of asceticism. To justify this, the doctrine presents the human body as inferior to the intellect and, in the most extreme views, as a centre of evil. This idea was certainly pervasive in Hellenic asceticism[131] and it greatly influenced the Early Fathers. But the Bible sees man and his body differently. Man is a unity; there are no parts in him that can be separated without losing the whole person. When reference is made to man's soul, spirit or heart – this latter term being the most often used – it refers to the intellectual faculty that enables him to think, reflect, understand and decide. Man is never presented as disembodied. Jesus is at all times present in the body, even after his death when he is described eating a piece of broiled fish[132]. His disciples saw him bodily ascending to the sky[133]. Even Lazarus and the rich man are described as having a body after their death[134]. I do not wish to speculate on what happens after death with our bodies, but mean simply to point out that a disembodied soul is certainly not a biblical view.

Next, we must consider man's sin. His body is never blamed for sinning, but his "heart" – i.e. his intellectual faculty – is. This is where the decisions about how he should live are made[135]. However, this raises a question. What about many NT passages where the flesh or parts of our body are indicated as the source of evil?[136] This can be explained by using the alcoholic as an illustration. An alcoholic's body craves for alcohol and drives him to drink even when he would prefer to stop. Therefore, because of this biological and psychological craving, one metaphorically may speak of the "desires of the flesh". But this is only a metaphorical expression; the Bible never blames the body for this craving but the heart. Just as the alcoholic's body is not to be blamed for his condition; the blame must be put on his decision to abuse drink in the first

---

[131] Grau, 2011
[132] Luke 24:36-43
[133] Acts 1:9
[134] Luke 16:19-31
[135] Proverbs 4:23
[136] Matthew 26:41; Romans 7:21-25; Galatians 5:17

place. To get rid of the addiction, the solution is not to destroy his body but for him to decide to stop drinking and thus heal his body. That is the biblical position and the meaning of the resurrection of the body.

The Hellenic viewed things in the reverse and blamed the body but acquitted the intellectual faculties. This had its origin in Plato who carried the idea further and divided likewise the world into two: one, an imperfect and changeable world we experienced with our senses – our body – and the other, a perfect and unchangeable world to which we have access through our intellect, which he identified with the soul. Rather than the intellect dragging the body down, as understood in the Bible, the soul is:

> ... dragged by the body into the region of the change-able, and wanders and is confused; the world spins round her [the soul], and she is like a drunkard... But when returning into herself she reflects, then she passes into the other world, the region of purity, and eternity, and immortality, and unchangeableness, which are her kindred, and with them she ever lives, when she is by herself and is not let or hindered; then she ceases from her erring ways...[137]

This dualism of two worlds and of a body and a separate soul became an integral part of the Hellenic mind. Under the influence of Eastern religions and philosophy, it reached extremes, such as found in Gnosticism, which regarded the body as evil. As we shall see in the next sections, Hellenic dualism must have immensely influenced Ignatius, judging by his attitudes towards the present life, marriage and freedom.

Life and Martyrdom

From the accounts of Ignatius' martyrdom one must conclude that he sought martyrdom almost of his own initiative. He even requested his friends in Rome not to intervene on his behalf. It is possible that some of them may have had suffi-

---

[137] Plato, 1999, p. 65

cient influence in Roman circles to save his life or even nego-tiate his freedom. But, he would have none of this:

> I write to the Churches, and impress on them all, that I shall willingly die for God, unless ye hinder me. I be-seech of you not to show an unseasonable good-will to-wards me. Suffer me to become food for the wild beasts, through whose instrumentality it will be granted me to attain to God. I am the wheat of God, and let me be ground by the teeth of the wild beasts, that I may be found the pure bread of Christ. Rather entice the wild beasts, that they may become my tomb, and may leave nothing of my body; so that when I have fallen asleep [in death], I may be no trouble to any one. Then shall I truly be a disciple of Christ, when the world shall not see so much as my body.[138]

We cannot deny Ignatius' enormous courage as shown in this passage. But we also note a degree of contempt for his body – wishing it to "be ground by the teeth of the wild beasts" – that far surpasses Plato and approaches that of Gnosticism. From here, it is natural that he should put his readers on guard against physical pleasures, especially sex and some other lusts. Thus, he praises celibacy, admittedly only in passing.

Celibacy and Marriage

We must examine this with some care and consider Ignatius' impact on our times as well as his, for celibacy and marriage have been controversial themes over the years. What follows may seem somewhat of a digression, but it is especially im-portant in our present times, given the confusion about what constitutes marriage and its function in society. Celibacy is still regarded by some as an instrument of getting closer to God and to please him more than is possible in married life. It is a requirement for monastic and clerical life in the Catholic

---

[138] Schaff, n.d.a., Epistle to the Romans, IV

church and other denominations. Nuns are regarded as "brides of Christ." Ignatius' words in question are:

> Honour those [who continue] in virginity, as the priest-esses of Christ; and the widows [that persevere] in gravity of behaviour, as the altar of God.[139]

Here again, one can detect Hellenic influences behind this passage. Celibacy was practised by Greek priests and some schools of philosophy; Rome venerated its Vestal virgins, who served as priestesses to the goddess Vesta. Ignatius' "priest-esses of Christ" suggest they were Christian counterparts. Yet there was another likely source, found in the seventh chapter of Paul's first letter to the Corinthians. To interpret its contents, it helps to have a clear view of what the OT taught about marriage. For whatever Paul said, it would have been in harmony with the OT[140]. Marriage was described as part of the Creation account in Genesis and was given three purposes: companionship, help with work and procreation of children. God created mankind as male and female, two creatures with different but complementary qualities.

The empirical evidence – whether biological, psychological, historical or sociological – points to the benefits of a lifelong union of man and woman. Man is not complete until he belongs to a woman and vice versa. When marriage is discarded by society, its first victims are women. For women, happiness is strongly dependent upon the emotional and loving environment that comes from her man. The OT law was both insightful and tender about this feminine trait; it required that, for a full year, a newly married man should be relieved of all work or military duty to allow him to stay at home with his wife and make her happy[141]. The cited objective of this leave is her happiness, not his. It also shows that the OT law was not always stern, there was a lot of softness in it as well.

---

[139] Schaff, n.d.a., Epistle to the Tarsians, IX
[140] Matthew 5:17
[141] Deuteronomy 24:5

Certainly, there are people who have no desire for marriage, but they are the exception. Most women today who are unmarried will admit that they are so because no man has asked them to marry. Men are less likely to reveal the reason for their being unmarried, but the reason is often that they want their freedom, that is, they are not prepared to commit themselves beyond their own selfish interests. Some are happy to live with a woman, not as their wife, but as a mistress.

Marriage is not only good for the couple, it is also good for society at large. It takes a man and a woman, united in body and soul by love and lifelong commitment, to produce children, educate them and prepare them for life as useful citizens. Marriage is working together – Eve was created as Adam's assistant[142]. When man and wife fulfil their common vision and vocation, the synergy of their love and skills far exceeds the capability of the single person.

Concerning sexual relations, the OT never described them as impure or even second best. On the contrary, the complete Song of Solomon was dedicated to the sensual joy of love. While condemning adultery and extramarital intercourse, the Bible encouraged a man to enjoy the physical love of his wife and vice versa[143]. Nowhere in the OT was celibacy advocated nor was it suggested that abstention from sex released a man from fleshly concerns in order to dedicate himself to purer pursuits[144].

Having clarified the OT view of marriage, we may now return to Paul. We must keep in mind when reading his letters that, although Paul was a gifted organiser of people, he was not such a good organiser of thoughts when writing. One should make allowance for his circumstances which kept him almost permanently on the move without the comfort of a desk and the possibility of several drafts. Apart from the lack of an

---

[142] Note that the reference to Eve as a helpmate appears shortly after Adam is put to work in the garden (Genesis 2:15 & 18).
[143] Proverbs 5:15-19
[144] It is interesting to note that following OT times, Judaism regarded marriage as a duty and celibacy as a sin (Kohler and Margolis, 1906).

orderly flow of ideas in Chapter 7[145], Paul was answering questions raised by the Corinthian church. We have no access to these questions, so we are deprived of the context of Paul's answers that may have helped us understand what he meant. There is one further complication, he admitted that part of the answers were the words of God and other answers were his own. Yet, he added that his words were inspired by the Spirit and thus ascribed a degree of authority to them, which leaves us wondering how much authority we should attribute to them.

Due to his claim to spiritual inspiration, some biblical commentators give as much weight to what Paul said as to God's words. I disagree with them. For we must make a difference between being a witness[146] of God and being inspired by God. In the Bible, a prophet or an apostle spoke with God's authority when he was a witness either to God's action or to His speech; both were treated as witnessing concrete historical events. In this way, the prophet simply communicated what he claimed to have seen or heard, full stop. Inspiration, on the other hand, while it may have been triggered by an observation, included the inspired person's own reflection, reasoning and evaluation. Although he may have been inspired by God, his own personal engagement may have somewhat distorted what had been inspired. He could not speak with God's authority because he was communicating something not witnessed or only partially witnessed. Thus, when Paul spoke from the knowledge that had been inspired by the Spirit, he spoke his own views, without the authority of a witness. And about marriage Paul had much to learn, for he was a bachelor[147]. So we

---

[145] 1 Corinthians 7

[146] Acts 1:8

[147] It may also be possible that his advice was directed to people who had to live like himself, travelling from one place to another and regularly having to face all kinds of adversities. No doubt the demands upon him were such that marriage and family were out of the question. He was given therefore, the ability to be content as an unmarried man (Matthew 19:12). Under similar circumstances, Jeremiah also had to forfeit marriage and family (Jeremiah 16:2-4).

must test the soundness of his ideas about it, as he himself would urge us[148].

Chapter seven in the first epistle to the Corinthians was divided into four parts. The first dealt with marriage as a way out of temptation and celibacy as a preferable option. The second part dealt with divorce – here we have no problems, for it is more or less a repetition of what Christ taught. The third part says nothing about marriage, so we may skip it. The fourth part returns to the subject of celibacy and marriage, so we may treat the first and last part together.

Two verses in both parts imply that Paul's words do not constitute commands but grant "permission" (v. 6) and reflect his "opinion" (v. 25). Whatever, he was in error and contradicted the OT teaching. He suggested people marry as an escape valve from sexual urges and from fornication; he did not mention love, shared calling and happiness. Sadly, because these words have not been critically considered, they are to this day strongly bound up with the church. For example, the marriage service of the Church of England Book of Common Prayer lists the second objective of marriage as follows:

> It was ordained for a remedy against sin, and to avoid fornication; that such persons as have not the gift of continency might marry, and keep themselves undefiled members of Christ's body.

One wonders how seriously these words have been taken, for I think most Christian people would object to one marrying to satisfy a sexual urge. But until recently[149], they were read at wedding ceremonies with great solemnity.

Later on (v. 33-35) Paul stated that a married person, in pleasing his spouse, showed care for the things of the world and not of God and implied that by marrying one neglected purity of body and spirit. This was not God's word, but the

---

[148] 1 Thessalonians 5:20-21
[149] New versions of the prayer book use more gentle wording; however the original prayer book still remains the standard of liturgy and creed for the Anglican church.

view of a man who, I have already said, has not been married.
It is true that normally young couples start by having eyes only
for each other. This is by no means wrong; on the contrary, it
is how purity of flesh, blood and soul become concrete in marriage. Falling in love and romance are God's idea and he added
in his Law a wedding gift: leave of absence for a one year hon-
eymoon. But after an initial period and the arrival of the first
child, things change. Children, especially when they are very
young, put a total and constant demand upon their parents.
This is a fine pedagogical tool of God, for it teaches a couple
how to put the needs of others ahead of their own. With time,
children's demands upon parents give them a parental outlook
on life that gradually extends beyond the immediate family to
the surrounding community and its needs. They learn the art of
exercising authority and responsibility. And as they grow, the
now not-so-young couple gradually become father and mother
not only to their children, but to others as well. Here we find
purity of body and soul – in practice rather than in mere words
– helping humanity overcome its vicissitudes.

I think Paul eventually learned this, either directly from
God or by his Spirit-guided observation of society[150]. In a letter to the Ephesians, written a couple of years later, he gave
marriage the highest regard by considering it a symbol of the
union between Christ and the church[151]. About eight to ten
years later he showed the practical side of this symbol. Writing
to Timothy and Titus, he categorically stated that leaders of the
church, whether elders or deacons, should be married to one
wife[152]. He must have also learned about the pedagogical value
of married life, for he set knowledge of how to lead a family
as the required qualification for these offices. Yet, regardless
of my critical comments on his early views on marriage, I hold
the greatest regard for Paul and respect his authority. At first, I
wished that Paul had delayed answering these questions from

---

[150] He must have been impressed with the functioning of couples such as
Aquila and Priscilla, who were real gems to him and the church (Romans
16: 3-5).
[151] Ephesians 5:31-32
[152] 1 Timothy 3:1-13; Titus 1:5-9

Corinth and had dealt with them somewhere else – without leaving a record. Yet, I gather that his answer must have been included in the letter for some purpose. It shows that Paul, despite being a "chosen vessel"[153] was a man like any other and held, when he was young, some ideas that needed further experience and testing. But he was an honest man and told us openly what came from God and what came from him. His honesty adds to the authenticity of the things he wrote as coming from God.

Slavery

Moved by his asceticism, Ignatius regarded the desire of a slave to be set free as an expression of lust:

> Let them not desire to be set free out of the common [fund], lest they be found the slaves of lust.[154]

We ought to start by clarifying the biblical position on slavery. Firstly, the bible went further than the modern concept of equality as worded, for example, in the USA Declaration of Independence as "all men are created equal". In the Bible, all men were created in the image of God, this added glory and honour to humanity which is omitted by mere equality. Secondly, no man could own another for all were owned by God who purchased them through Christ[155]. Thirdly, as we have already stated, the whole thrust of the Bible was the emancipation of humanity from all forms of bondage and it was the duty of God's people to put the process into action. Paul's letter to Philemon attests to this when he entreated him to receive his slave Onesimus as a brother rather than a slave[156]. We read in between the lines in Ignatius' critical letter to Polycarp that the church in Smyrna had used its funds to pay for the re-

---

[153] Acts 9:15
[154] Schaff, n.d.a., Epistle to Polycarp, IV
[155] Acts 20:28; 1 Corinthians 6:19-20; Ephesians 1:7. By this was meant that Christ had paid the purchase price that released a man from bondage to evil.
[156] Philemon 1:15-16

lease of slaves. Yet Ignatius attempted to obstruct the effort of the church fulfilling its emancipatory agenda. This revealed a lack of understanding of the concreteness of the biblical message, that is, that Christ endeavoured to free the whole of man and not just his soul.

Summary

Ignatius' letters reveal an inflexible and ascetic man. He supported an episcopal system that granted authority to the bishop that went far beyond that granted in the NT. It was not beneficial for the educational development of a community. His praise of martyrdom for martyrdom's sake, and celibacy, laid on people's backs burdens that were not demanded by Scripture. It undervalued the giving of life by the Spirit and the immense worth of marriage dedicated to the service of God and the community. His views on emancipation had not yet caught the full biblical thrust. His views of the episcopacy began the transition from community to bureaucracy and his asceticism lost the view of true goodness (see Table 3-1). But Ignatius also left us a positive legacy. His being prepared to sacrifice his life for his faith was based on the conviction of Christ's resurrection. One may argue that some people who were martyrs were naive, but the man who wrote these letters was no fool. His acceptance of Christ's resurrection as an event witnessed by people whom he must have personally met significantly adds to the historical solidity of the Christian faith.

5 Justin Martyr

Undervaluing of the OT, as discussed in the prior chapter, went beyond having an impact on the way people read the NT. It also allowed a man like Justin to be uncritical about the way of thinking that he had inherited from Hellenism in his effort to develop a Christian philosophy. Justin's philosophical orientation changed several times during his life; he began as a Stoic, then moved on to Aristotle and finally, prior to his conversion to Christianity, reached Plato. As we indicated in the previous chapter, Plato's thought and as we gather from the following passage, the physical world was for him imperfect and always changing, while the world of ideas was perfect and thus unchanging:

> That which is apprehended by intelligence and reason is always in the same state; but that which is conceived by opinion with the help of sensation and without reason, is always in a process of becoming and perishing and never really is.[157]

Naturally, Plato's reasoning needed only to apprehend a static world and therefore was itself static and far more simple than the reasoning required to comprehend a dynamic world. Since people live in a world that is always changing, we can readily see that Plato's thinking, although showing a great degree of wisdom, fell short of the intellectual demands that a dynamic world imposed upon him. And here is the trap into which Justin fell. He attempted to explain the historical events of Jesus' life by transferring them from their dynamic setting into the static world of ideas. As a result, his Christian philosophy was inadequate; it was like expecting someone to watch a movie by looking at photographs of some of its scenes. It failed because a vast amount of information was lost[158]. And more specifically, it transformed the understanding of biblical truth into orthodoxy, something rigid and of limited relevance to life.

---

[157] Plato, 2008
[158] The study of information loss is one of the topics of cybernetics; an extended discussion of this is given in J. D. R. de Raadt, 2015.

The Logos

The door that Justin opened for the Greek idea of truth to enter Christian thinking was the *Logos*. *Logos* is one of those Greek words that we have alluded to as having two meanings and which must be understood in a Hebrew context, especially as used by John in the first verse of his Gospel:

> In the beginning was the Word [Logos], and the Word [Logos] was with God, and the Word [Logos] was God.

The introduction of the word *Logos* three times in just one sentence suggests John wished to leave no doubt in our minds that he was speaking of "the word of the Lord" as found in the OT. Except for Moses, no one in the OT ever saw God face to face[159], other prophets only heard his voice. When God approached a prophet, he came to him as "the word of the Lord"[160]. Therefore, God's word in the OT stands for God himself. Moreover, not everyone in the OT could listen to God's voice, only prophets and other members of Israel's leadership had such direct access. But now, says John, all this has been changed and the voice of God – God himself – has become an historical man[161], the man Jesus Christ. Everyone who saw him in the flesh met God, man to man and they became the historical witnesses to the event[162]. It is in this context that we must understand Jesus' words "I am the truth"[163], truth becomes materialised in the historical and empirical events of his life. Those events are then integrated into our lives, so that from then on "to live is Christ"[164]. This demands that we live historically active lives, shaped by Christ's own life and by exercising historical reasoning[165].

---

[159] Exodus 33:11
[160] See for example 1 Samuel 3:7; Jeremiah 1:4; Ezekiel 1:3
[161] John 1:14
[162] Acts 1:8
[163] John 14:6
[164] Philippians 1:21
[165] For a detailed discussion of historical reasoning refer to J. D. R. de Raadt, 2013, p. 50-57.

The *Logos* of the Greek philosophers was something altogether different. The term was first used by Heraclitus as an ultimate truth that was behind everything that happened. Although Plato and Aristotle did not refer to *Logos* in the same way, they used the word *Eidos* – a form or model God applied to produce the world – to convey a similar idea. The Stoics believed *Logos* to be a universal principle that stood behind all things. Yet, regardless of these differences all these philosophers had a metaphysical objective in their inquires. I mean by this that they were searching for some principle that stood behind the physical and historical reality of our world and that although it was not a part of it, it ordered and ruled it. They assumed that this principle was pure static reason – reason narrowly circumscribed to logic and mathematics – and they called it *Logos* or *Eidos*. Their *Logos* or *Eidos* had no conception of the historical drama of man's predicament as found in the Bible.

The metaphysical pursuit of understanding has always proven an impossible task. It resembles what monkeys do when they are handed a mirror. They look behind the mirror to find the face reflected in it, but they find nothing. Through this illustration I do not mean to offend either ancient or modern philosophers. Though some scholars would pursue a metaphysical idea purely as an end in itself[166], I realise that others are driven by more serious concerns. The latter realise that their science lacks an essential element that ought to link together all the scientific bits and pieces into a unified whole and provide an overall purpose to it. Therefore, they engage in a metaphysical quest to find this essential unifying element. But it only amounts to looking behind the mirror. Much scientific endeavour is wasted, although it is desperately needed by people living in misery on this side of the mirror, where Christ stood.

---

[166] Paul encountered some Epicureans and Stoics in Athens who engaged in this pastime, see Acts 17:18-21.

Despite all this, Justin set out to connect the Greek *Logos* with the biblical one[167] and thus provide a metaphysical explanation of Christ. His effort amounted to reversing the incarnation, a well intended but fruitless project. It was also unnecessary. When the apostles set out to accomplish the mission that Christ had entrusted them with, they carried it out by giving an account of the historical events they had witnessed and the meaning of these events in the lives of men and women. Without any resort to metaphysics, they touched people of all walks of life, Jews and Gentiles, educated and uneducated. Their accounts were eventually written into the Gospels that we have today and these have not stopped touching people's lives for two millenniums.[168] There is no reason to doubt that this apostolic approach, so effective in the first century, could be carried on as effectively in the second century and thereafter.

Unfortunately, Justin opened a Pandora's box out of which sprang a string of convoluted concepts that generated long debates. Eventually, these settled into orthodoxy, that is, fixed statements of "right doctrine" expressed in a framework of thought foreign to the Bible. Let us examine what Justin had to say about the Logos:

> ...this power which the prophetic word calls God... was begotten from the Father, by His power and will, but not by abscission, as if the essence of the Father were divided; as all other things partitioned and divided are not the same after as before they were divided... [but as] fires kindled from a fire, which we see to be distinct from it, and yet that from which many can be kindled is by no means made less, but remains the same...[169]

---

[167] The Jewish philosopher, Philo of Alexandria, attempted it earlier on and may have had some influence on Justin.

[168] Interestingly, the most historically detailed and most beautifully written account – including the book of Acts – came from the hand of Luke, probably a Gentile rather than a Jew. The Church Fathers ought to have emulated his way of thinking.

[169] Schaff, n.d.a., Dialogue with Trypho, CXXVIII

It is hard to imagine that ordinary people living in the second century – or for that matter in the 21st century – would have been able to make any sense of this. What would "abscission", "essence" and "partitioned" mean to them? Despite such confusion, I must concede that Justin made a positive contribution to Christian thought by stating the universality of truth in the Logos, i.e., all truth resides in and is provided by Christ. This is something that the Christian humanists took up again in the Renascence and it provided an impetus for the development of the humanities incorporating the Greek philosophers' unique contribution to the humanities and natural sciences.

The Lord's Supper

Prior to his execution, Christ celebrated the traditional passover meal, which was a re-enactment of the last meal that Israel ate before leaving Egypt[170]. It was a family meal at which its members ate a lamb without blemish and with its blood they marked the posts and lintel of the entrance door to their homes. It took place in people's homes, not in the temple. It was to be a reminder of the night when God judged Egypt and when every first born belonging to a home not marked with the lamb's blood was stricken dead. The Israelites were no better as people than the Egyptians, yet they were spared from judgement by the blood smeared at their door. The punishment for their sins had been symbolically borne by the sacrificial lamb. Thus, they were commanded to celebrate this meal once a year forever after, so they would be reminded of this most momentous event in Israel's history that marked its birth as a nation chosen by God. Everything had to be replicated in the same manner. The complete procedure was symbolic of the historical circumstances they were re-enacting: the judgement, the redemption from Israel's oppressors, the payment of sins by innocent life, the provision of the lamb's meat for food and the haste of the meal taken before their flight. It was a memorial celebration with a pedagogical purpose; when in the fu-

---

[170] Exodus 12:1-27

ture, children should ask why they were eating in such a manner, they were to be taught about this historical event and its significance in their lives. As we have already said, the Hebrew people thought on the basis of their history and not by the cause and effect logic of the Greeks.

On the night that he was betrayed, Jesus celebrated this meal with his disciples. While they were still eating, that is, during the meal, he gave them bread and wine, telling them that these symbolised his body which would be sacrificed the next day – in place of the lamb. The wine symbolised his blood, the blood of the covenant[171]. Everything pointed to an historical progression that began with the covenant God made with Abraham. It specified that his descendants would become a nation[172] blessed by God and that it would be a blessing to all people. This covenant was honoured when God liberated Israel from the yoke of Egypt and established it as a free kingdom. The next historical step was accomplished by God sending his Messiah to liberate Israel once more and restore it as a kingdom. A lamb had to be sacrificed again and that lamb was Jesus himself. The bread and the wine were an addition to the rest of the passover meal and were meant to be a memorial[173] of how God once again fulfilled his covenant. It was celebrated thus while the apostles were alive[174] and most certainly took place in a home[175], for the church owned no buildings. Most likely children asked questions and they would have listened to an account of these historical events and their significance in their lives.

We must now return to Justin and examine what he had to say about this meal:

---

[171] Exodus 24:8; Matthew 26:28
[172] Genesis 12:2
[173] 1 Corinthians 11:24-25. The Greek word *anamnesis* (G364) in the original, commonly translated as *remembrance*, means *recollection*. It is very similar to the Hebrew word zikrown (H2146) used in Exodus 12:14 and *mnemósunon* (G3422) used in its Greek Septuagint version.
[174] 1 Corinthians 11:20; *deipnon* (G1173), usually translated as supper stands for the main meal of the day.
[175] Acts 2:46

> ...this food is called among us Εὐχαριστία [the Euchar-
> ist][176]... not as common bread and common drink do we
> receive these; but in like manner as Jesus Christ our Sa-
> viour, having been made flesh by the Word of God, had
> both flesh and blood for our salvation, so likewise have
> we been taught that the food which is blessed by the
> prayer of His word, and from which our blood and flesh
> by transmutation are nourished, is the flesh and blood
> of that Jesus who was made flesh.[177]

While ordinary parents and their children would have understood the narration of historical events, such as the Exodus,
and of Christ's crucifixion, I doubt that they would have been
able to make sense of a word such as "transmutation". Why the
change of name from Lord's Supper to Eucharist? Why go
beyond the understandable reality of history into metaphysics
which requires specialised knowledge?

This specialised knowledge perfectly fitted Weber's model
of bureaucracy. Justin's philosophy amounted to an invitation
for people with a bureaucratic bent of mind to appropriate it,
turn it into some job specification and then create the appropriate role to perform it. As we shall see, this is what happened.

Worship

We stated earlier on that a bureaucracy provides a material
or non-material service. Judging by the following account,
already by the middle of the second century we have the beginnings of this service:

> ... on the day called Sunday, all who live in cities or in
> the country gather together to one place, and the mem-
> oirs of the apostles or the writings of the prophets are
> read, as long as time permits; then, when the reader has
> ceased, the president verbally instructs, and exhorts to

---

[176] *Eucharistía* means thanksgiving and is used several times in the NT,
but never to refer to the Lord's Supper. It must be noted however that
Justin was not the first to use this term; it is presumed to have been used
in an earlier writing, Richardson, n.d., Didaché 9.
[177] Schaff, n.d.a., The First Apology, LXVI

> the imitation of these good things. Then we all rise to-
> gether and pray, and, as we before said, when our
> prayer is ended, bread and wine and water are brought,
> and the president in like manner offers prayers and
> thanksgivings, according to his ability, and the people
> assent, saying Amen; and there is a distribution to each,
> and a participation of that over which thanks have been
> given, and to those who are absent a portion is sent by
> the deacons[178].

This passage has been lauded by low church Christians as
providing a precedent for simple rather than elaborate worship;
this should be noted as they have identified this as worship.
Subtle, yet significant changes can be detected in Justin's account. Justin tells us that they gathered at "one place", most
unlikely to be a home[179]. This may explain why only bread and
wine were served and not a meal. At least symbolically, eliminating the meal severs the historical connection between the
passover of the OT and Christ's death. Hellenic Christians had
little knowledge of OT history and the background it was to
Christ's life, so an opportunity to learn about it was missed.
Then, the roles played by a "president" and the deacons in
conducting this gathering, plus the selection of the day which
had a specific meaning – Sunday and Christ's resurrection –
give an aura of formality to the gathering.

These are the beginnings of the worship service and a
"Christian liturgical practice"[180] that became the highest point
of Christian activity[181]. And one may conclude that the president and the deacons are the predecessors to a professional

---

[178] Schaff, n.d.a., The First Apology LXVII
[179] A description of these gatherings in a letter from Pliny to the emperor
Trajan – at the beginning of the second century – indicates that such gatherings took place at dawn and, given the description, it is unlikely that the
people assembled in a home.
[180] Bruce, 1970, p. 171
[181] This is the reverse of what Christ taught the Samaritan woman (John
4:21-23). For a discussion of this passage see J. D. R. de Raadt, 2013, p.
80f.

clergy operating in an ecclesiastical bureaucracy. The work of the laity slid quietly into the background.

Community

Yet these developments were still in the future; we may gather from Justin that the sense of a Christian community with a social and civic concern was still existent at the time:

> [We]...follow the only unbegotten God through His Son – we who formerly delighted in fornication, but now embrace chastity alone; we who formerly used magical arts, dedicate ourselves to the good and unbegotten God; we who valued above all things the acquisition of wealth and possessions, now bring what we have into a common stock, and communicate to every one in need; we who hated and destroyed one another, and on account of their different manners would not live with men of a different tribe, now, since the coming of Christ, live familiarly with them, and pray for our enemies, and endeavour to persuade those who hate us unjustly to live conformably to the good precepts of Christ, to the end that they may become partakers with us of the same joyful hope of a reward from God the ruler of all.[182]

It could be argued that Justin is writing in defence of Christians and therefore shows only their better side in order to avoid their persecution[183]. Nevertheless, it is a testimony that Christians had high standards of conduct and practised social justice which must have been sufficiently adhered to for Justin to raise them in their defence. This is no meagre achievement. One must consider that the Israelites[184] were rather straightlaced when compared with their neighbours, including the Hellenic world of Justin's time. They had a strict law that

---

[182] Schaff, n.d.a., The First Apology XIV

[183] Although an earlier letter of Pliny, 2013, to the emperor Trajan gives a description of Christians that partly concurs with the writing of Justin.

[184] I use the term Israelite broadly, which includes the Jewish people after the kingdoms of Israel and Judah had disappeared.

covered every aspect of their lives and there was always a Rabbi or other such leader to impress it upon them. Certainly, there were deviances and dissipations, but the influence for this came from outside their community rather than from inside.

The early church inherited these standards and even more, for Christ demanded his people to walk "the extra mile"[185]. It set a heavy load upon the apostles' shoulders to teach this to new converts when they moved out of their familiar Jewish territory into the Hellenic world of the Mediterranean. Paul's epistles to the Corinthian church is a good illustration of the tensions that sprang up between the apostle and newly converted gentiles. Undoubtedly the gentile world had its great moralists such as Socrates, Aristotle and the Stoics; nevertheless, their standards belonged to the social elite and not to the common people. Yet it was these who needed such standards the most; they were hit the hardest by ignorance, dissipation, abuse of children, incest and the prostitution of young girls[186]. But in contrast to the Greek philosophers, the OT claimed that God was on the side of the poor rather than the rich. Christ insisted that he came to heal the sick and not the healthy; to pull the poor out of the dunghill and turn them into a nobility[187].

We are indebted to Justin for this account. He provided us with evidence that, judging by the way these people lived, they still understood that the church was meant to be a community. But, by introducing abstract thinking into plain historical facts, he also helped transform a vision of society into theological formulas that eventually became regarded as orthodox. He also began lifting worship above lay work (see Table 3-1).

---

[185] Matthew 5:41
[186] Schaff, n.d.a., The First Apology XXVII
[187] 1 Samuel 2:8, Luke 1:52; Matthew 9:12

6 Irenaeus

Introduction

The kind of speculative approach in which Justin engaged was not an isolated instance but formed part of the broad philosophical and religious interests that characterised his times. Many people with such interests embraced Christianity but at the same time carried into their new creed their earlier intellectual and religious outlook generating, as a result, their own versions of Christianity. Gnosticism in particular – an eclectic approach to religion and philosophy that mixed ideas from all parts of the Mediterranean and Eastern world – went a long way in its attempt to redefine the Christian faith. As an example of gnostic writing, we might consider the opening passage of one of its own gospels:

> The gospel of truth is joy to those who have received from the Father of truth the gift of knowing him by the power of the Logos, who has come from the Pleroma and who is in the thought and the mind of the Father; he it is who is called "the Saviour," since that is the name of the work which he must do for the redemption of those who have not known the Father. For the name of the gospel is the manifestation of hope, since that is the discovery of those who seek him, because the All sought him from whom it had come forth. You see, the All had been inside of him, that illimitable, inconceivable one, who is better than every thought.[188]

We need not immerse ourselves into an inquiry of what is meant by "the Pleroma", "the All" or the "that illimitable, inconceivable one". They are a sample of purely speculative ideas, foreign to the Hebrew mind and that have neither application to everyday life nor is their esoteric language intelligible. Nevertheless, we may well ask to what extent did Justin's speculations about the Logos, also written in rather

---

[188] The Nag Hammadi Library, 1984

convoluted words, encourage gnostic people to meddle with Christianity? Yet, Justin's philosophy was generally accepted while gnosticism was fiercely rejected.

The Rule of Truth

The man who took up the task of repulsing the gnostic teaching was Irenaeus and he undertook this task with the utmost energy. He particularly targeted Valentinus who is considered the possible author of *The Gospel of Truth*. We are not as much interested in the content of Irenaeus' argumentation against Valentinus, as we are in the path he followed to build his argument. This path is graphically set out in Figure 6-1 starting from the historical events described in the Bible and ending with the orthodox "rule of truth"[189] with which Irenaeus fought gnosticism.

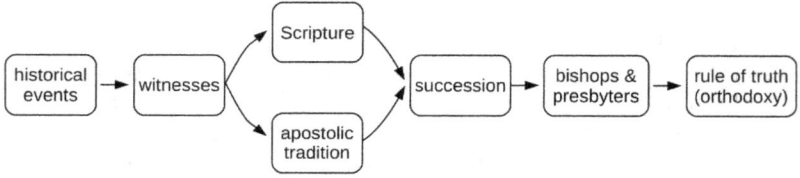

Figure 6-1 From Events to "Rule of Truth"

We have already explained that Scripture is the record of witnesses to historical events written down by people who had an historical way of thinking. But in addition to Scripture, Irenaeus refers to "traditions" and his text is not clear as to whether he uses the word as a synonym to Scripture or whether it refers to something not contained in Scripture but of equal validity. Reflecting their differences regarding doctrinal authority, Protestants tend to assume the former and Catholics the latter. The ambiguity of Irenaeus' usage of the term, added to the unreliable versions of his work available to us, makes it difficult to decide for the one or the other, from an impartial point of view. Reading the text we have at hand one gets the

---

[189] Schaff, n.d.a., Against Heresies, III, XI, 1

impression that he used the terms interchangeably. However, if we are to follow Irenaeus' path to truth, the determining factor is the succession as he defined it in the following passage:

> ...it is incumbent to obey the presbyters who are in the Church, – those who, as I have shown, possess the succession from the apostles; those who, together with the succession of the episcopate, have received the certain gift of truth, according to the good pleasure of the Father. But [it is also incumbent] to hold in suspicion others who depart from the primitive succession, and assemble themselves together in any place whatsoever, [looking upon them] either as heretics of perverse minds, or as schismatics puffed up and self-pleasing, or again as hypocrites, acting thus for the sake of lucre and vainglory. For all these have fallen from the truth.[190]

Irenaeus is telling us that any material regarded as truth, whether in the Bible or otherwise, must have been transmitted by a legitimate channel which he terms a "succession". The transmission of knowledge from one generation to another is no monopoly of the church. Most of science is indeed a chain of knowledge that is passed from one scholar to another. But Irenaeus institutionalised this chain; only some people – bishops and presbyters – were suitably accredited by the "succession" of their office to transfer the truth. In other words, he bureaucratised truth, by affixing it to the appropriate officers of the church[191]. He removed Christian thought from the people and regarded only these officers as being authorised to think. Engaging in thought by unauthorised people, even if they were not gnostic, classified them as "heretics of perverse mind" or "schismatics". In addition to his lengthy arguments

---

[190] Schaff, n.d.a., Against Heresies, IV, XXVI, 2; bracketed inserts added by the translator.

[191] I must nevertheless acknowledge a positive contribution from Irenaeus. In his efforts to legitimise church teachings according to succession, he accredited most of the books of the NT. That is, they were regarded in his time as records of material originating from people who had witnessed the life of Christ and the early mission of the church.

against gnostic ideas, he had this second weapon: ordinary people were not authorised to think.

Critical and Creative Thinking

No doubt Irenaeus was effective in combating the absurd speculations of gnosticism, but while battling them he also delivered two heavy blows to the Christian intellect. The first blow removed critical thinking and discernment of character behind this thinking. Critical thinking does not mean that we should only look at the logical consistency of thought. Thought is always dependent on faith – faith in God and faith in other people. We simply cannot check all the knowledge necessary for living, we must also rely upon the trustworthiness of the people who have generated such knowledge. This entails our evaluating their character and even more importantly, evaluating the outcomes that flow out of their thought when applied. For a tree ought to be judged by its fruit[192]. Thus, we first believe in the Gospels and in the Jesus they describe because other people believe in them. But this does not preclude us, as our thoughts and faith mature, to be able to evaluate by ourselves the historical consistency of the Gospels, the character of their writers and the impact that their message – their fruit – had on society. Yet, we will always remain indebted to others who are not necessarily bishops or presbyters, but simply ordinary people like parents, friends and teachers. We might be even indebted to people whom we never met but only read or of whom we were told about. These were people who Irenaeus wished to disenfranchise.

Irenaeus' second blow was aimed at creative thinking and faith. The events recorded in the Bible provide us with an historical thrust, an ever-widening civic vision and thought, aimed at addressing the predicament of humanity. This needs professional skills; skills in turn require knowledge, specifically the knowledge encased in the natural and human sciences. These skills and knowledge were seen as integral to revelation.

---

[192] Matthew 7:18

The arts revealed by the Holy Spirit were to be used for the benefit of all people. Rather than conforming to the pattern of the times[193], Christians were meant to renew their minds and attain the "mind of Christ"[194] by organising all knowledge to accomplish his mission[195]. The arts were necessary to bring a transformation of self, that is, to make them citizens of God's city. In addition, Christians also needed them to "...repair the waste cities..." and civilise the Roman world[196]. That was their mission at that time.

Bureaucracy

Irenaeus on the other hand, was mostly concerned with tradition and orthodoxy. Like other earlier Church Fathers, his interest was in Christianity as a religion. Like them, he was committed to evangelising people, but neglected civilising them. Rather than educating them and teaching them to think, he would indoctrinate them and to do this he endorsed a bureaucratic structure of bishops and presbyters. Thus, less than a century after the apostolic era, the church had abandoned its communal structure and donned the mantle of an institution divided into an ordained clergy and a laity. The former provided the service, the latter played the role of clients. Christianity for the laity was no longer a mission to change the world – removing the arts from the reach of Christ would have sufficiently incapacitated them to do that – but a religion circumscribed to their personal lives. For them, changing the world was now limited to proselytising others and inducing them to doing the same. This was a blow from which the church, except for a comparably brief period in history, has never been fully able to recover.

Bureaucracies seek to centralise, they centralise themselves and they pressure society to centralise with them. They are one of the most powerful drivers behind a metropolis. The church

---

[193] Romans 12:2
[194] 1 Corinthians 2:16
[195] 2 Corinthians 10:5
[196] Isaiah 61:4

already appears to be no exception to this centralising process, for Irenaeus singles out:

> ... that tradition derived from the apostles, of the very great, the very ancient, and universally known Church founded and organised at Rome by the two most glorious apostles, Peter and Paul...[197]

Why did he not honour the more deserving church of Antioch instead? It was the first Christian seat of missions and the mother church of all churches in the Mediterranean world. It was also the oldest after Jerusalem. We may assume that Antioch, not being the centre of the empire, did not have the prestige of Rome and that Irenaeus assumed that such prestige had also rubbed on to the church there. He lent a helping hand to turn the Roman church into a bureaucratic hegemony in control of orthodoxy and indoctrination (see Table 3-1). It was a bureaucracy fashioned "according to this world"[198], regardless of how dysfunctional this world was.

---

[197] Schaff, n.d.a., Against Heresies, III, III, 2
[198] Romans 12:2

7 Tertullian

We now move to the beginning of the third century and meet Tertullian. There are two stages in Tertullian's thought. The first one followed Irenaeus in the fight against gnosticism. This is his apologetic work which has a strong legal flavour. Some have speculated that this was due to him being a lawyer, but this has not been established for certain. What is certain however is that what showed up was an accomplished bureaucratic mind, which is not surprising because bureaucracy and the practice of the law – as distinct from justice – walk hand in hand. Tertullian was also a strict ascetic; his fervour for asceticism bordered on fanaticism and matched Ignatius' devotion to martyrdom. Understandingly, he emerges as a rather unpopular character whose thinking has been described as:

> ...pharisaic and not Christian. It is profoundly religious, but the religion is not that of Jesus or of Paul. There is tremendous rugged strength in Tertullian, but it is a pagan moral energy. He had a vision of the living God, but he had not seen him in the face of Jesus Christ. He bowed in lovely reverence before God, but it was as a Judge and Master not as a Father and Friend.[199]

"Pharisaic" is a good description; like the Pharisees, he had a tendency to fight evil by issuing instructions to circumvent it rather than confront it head on. And like them, he liked to control the behaviour of people by setting down rigid laws of orthodoxy, which he termed "prescriptions"[200].

But in mid-life he underwent a change of heart and embraced the cause of the Montanists, a group of Christians who resembled the modern Charismatic movement. They claimed to have regained the earlier inspiration of the Holy Spirit – experienced during the apostolic era – and had received from him new revelations that were referred to as "new prophecy". Tertullian embraced this new prophecy and, although he did not depart from most orthodox teachings, he adopted its extreme ascetic practices. Therefore, one must differentiate

---

[199] D'Souza, 2005, p. 79
[200] For example, Schaff, n.d.c., Anti-Marcion, I

between the young Tertullian and the older one in outlining the main characteristics of his thought.

Work, Education and Idolatry

Like Paul and the rest of the Bible, idolatry for Tertullian was anything that subjected man to bondage, whether it be statues of gods, their temples or just immaterial things such as covetousness[201]. He regarded the evil of idolatry with the utmost seriousness and as "[the] principal crime of the human race, the highest guilt charged upon the world, the whole procuring cause of judgement..."[202] But in contrast to Paul, his way of handling idolatry was typically pharisaical; he did not deal with idolatry but totally withdrew from anything to do with it.

Paul regarded idols as products of the human imagination. Thus people like him, who regarded idols as mere fantasy, were free to ignore them and any object associated with them. They were free for example to eat meat sacrificed to idols, even inside a temple[203]. But he had a caring concern for people who were still influenced in some way by idolatry. He therefore cautioned people to be mindful of the impact their behaviour might have on their weaker brothers. His approach was to balance personal freedom with social responsibility. However, Tertullian cared little for freedom and ruled out-of-bounds everything associated with idols, even when regarded as totally fictional. He thus wiped out one of the most precious gifts that Christ endowed upon humanity: the freedom to act according to one's conscience. He also set the precedent that encouraged church leadership to become increasingly despotic, not only over Christians, but upon society as a whole.[204]

---

[201] Colossians 3:5; Philippians 3:19; Schaff, n.d.c., On Idolatry, XI

[202] Schaff, n.d.c., On Idolatry, XI, 1

[203] 1 Corinthians 8:1-13

[204] Thus when the French revolutionaries in 1879 cried "liberté, fraternité, equalité", they were rebelling against ecclesiastical and aristocratic despotism. But they were ignorant that the liberty that was a novelty to them had been proclaimed by Jesus eighteen centuries earlier.

Covetousness and gluttony were not vices practised only in antiquity, they are also very relevant topics for today, if we judge by our contemporary greed for money, the popularity of TV food shows and the obesity of a large proportion of modern people. This form of idolatry subtly enslaves through fear; for fear of loss is often a greater motivation for greed that a simple desire for more. Moreover, covetousness and gluttony make people vulnerable, they can be easily manipulated and exploited. We are interested therefore in knowing how to deal with this form of idolatry. Paul exhorted his people not to conform to the pattern of the world but to be transformed by the renewal of their minds, that is, by education.[205] This would ensure their freedom. But he did not encourage people to withdraw from the world; on the contrary just as Christ had taught, he realised the importance of constructively engaging in the world[206].

Tertullian did not capture the potential of engagement, he searched for any available detour that would avoid the perils of idolatry. Unfortunately, the path he found also neutralised any potential Christian influence in the affairs of society. More than that, he allowed them to place themselves in comfortable and sheltered positions where they could not do much wrong but neither could they do much good. For example, given the need of people to earn a living, he advised craftsmen to supply luxury goods for which there was a substantial demand and ample income to be made:

> If the necessity of maintenance is urged..., the arts have other species withal to afford means of livelihood, without outstepping the path of discipline, that is, without the... [false belief in]... an idol... Luxury and ostentation have more votaries than all superstition. Ostentation will require dishes and cups more easily than superstition. Luxury deals in wreaths, also, more than ceremony. ...therefore, we urge men generally to such

---

[205] Romans 12:2; John 8:32
[206] Matthew 5:13-14, 1 Corinthians 5:9-10; Philippians 2:15;

> kinds of handicrafts as do not come in contact with an idol...[207]

Tertullian's advice was certainly not the idea of work we introduced earlier on. Work for him was chiefly a means to earn a living and he disregarded the practical side of the vision that Christ entrusted to his followers. He did this by creating a grey "secular" space wedged between idolatry and true spirituality where the laity could look after their own interests without contaminating themselves with idolatry. He dealt with intellectual matters, specifically reading and teaching, in the same manner:

> We know it may be said, "If teaching literature is not lawful to God's servants, neither will learning be likewise;" and, "How could one be trained unto ordinary human intelligence, or unto any sense or action whatever, since literature is the means of training for all life? How do we repudiate *secular* studies, without which divine studies cannot be pursued?" Let us see, then, the necessity of literary erudition; let us reflect that partly it cannot be admitted, partly cannot be avoided. Learning literature is allowable for believers, rather than teaching; for the principle of learning and of teaching is different. If a believer teach literature, while he is teaching doubtless he commends, while he delivers he affirms, while he recalls he bears testimony to, the praises of idols interspersed therein.[208]

In this passage Tertullian acknowledged that there was useful learning that originated from outside God's special revelation to the prophets and apostles. In this he agreed with Justin. But he differed from him by regarding this learning as "secular", that is, as obtained independently from Christ. Justin, on the other hand, claimed that Christ was the source of all truth. For example, the truth that Socrates taught – and which Tertul-

---

[207] Schaff, n.d.c., On Idolatry, VIII
[208] Schaff, n.d.c., On Idolatry, X, emphasis added

lian would have considered as "secular" – was, according to Justin, delivered to Socrates by Christ[209].

We should note the manner in which Tertullian circumvented the problem of literature written by pagans. To avoid promoting the pagan gods referred in it, he allowed Christians to read it in order to learn for themselves but at the same time prohibited them from teaching it to others. It meant that Christians could learn for their own benefit without regard to the ignorance of others. But, by doing this, they hindered the effectiveness of improving society through education. Thirteen centuries later, the Christian humanists showed greater shrewdness and did more for education. Despite the shortage of good literature produced during the middle ages, the humanists were able to use the classical literature of Greece for the benefit of education by treating Homer's Olympian gods as mere fictional characters, no different to the talking animals of Aesop's fables.

Institutional Church

The grey "secular" sector, within which Christian participation was to be tolerated as a second best, functioned like a moat protecting a castle. It was the buffer zone, occupied by the laity, shielding the church from being "contaminated" by idolatry[210]. Sheltered behind this buffer zone were "their superiors" – the "clerical rank"[211] – ordained with such special powers that made it incumbent for the laity to show "reverence and modesty" towards them[212]. Laymen were only allowed to operate beyond this grey sector when clergy were not available. The "Eucharist", for example, had to be taken "... from the hand of none but the presidents..."[213]. Tertullian was highly critical of any laxity in this matter:

---

[209] This view was also held by the Christian humanists of the Renascence, including Erasmus. See J. D. R. de Raadt, 2013, p. 68-70.
[210] Schaff, n.d.c., On Idolatry, VII
[211] Schaff, n.d.d., On Monogamy, XII
[212] Schaff, n.d.c., On Baptism, XVII
[213] Schaff, n.d.c., The Chaplet, III

> Their ordinations, are carelessly administered, capricious, changeable. At one time they put novices in office; at another time, men who are bound to some secular employment... And so it comes to pass that to-day one man is their bishop, to-morrow another; to-day he is a deacon who to-morrow is a reader; to-day he is a presbyter who to-morrow is a layman. For even on laymen do they impose the functions of priesthood.[214]

It is likely that what appeared to Tertullian to be organisational chaos was the mere flexibility that a changing environment demanded of the church, which as we have seen, is an indispensable quality of a viable community. But Tertullian, with his bureaucratic turn of mind, avidly pursued institutional rigidity rather than flexibility. He also barred the clergy from "secular employment" and shaped a career for them by organising their ecclesiastical tasks[215]:

> ...[regarding] the due observance of giving and receiving baptism..., the chief priest (who is the bishop) has the right: in the next place, the presbyters and deacons, yet not without the bishop's authority, on account of the honour of the Church, which being preserved, peace is preserved.[216]

This excluded the work of the laity for it did not quite qualify as "good". Good works for Tertullian were ethereal and had limited, if any, practical benefit to society:

> We are the true adorers and the true priests, who, praying in spirit, sacrifice... [prayer in spirit]... – a victim proper and acceptable to God, which assuredly He has required, which He has looked forward to for Himself! This victim, devoted from the whole heart, fed on faith, tended by truth, entire in innocence, pure in chastity,

---

[214] Schaff, n.d.c., Anti-Marcion, I, XLI

[215] According to Weber, 2009, the work of a bureaucrat should be his sole occupation and be treated as his career.

[216] Schaff, n.d.c., On Baptism, XVII; He also makes reference to "the ministry of a priest ordained (to his sacred office)" in Schaff, n.d.d., On Exhortation to Chastity, XI

garlanded with love, we ought to escort with the pomp
of good works, amid psalms and hymns, unto God's altar, to obtain for us all things from God.[217]

Nor does the word "sacrifice" in the passage above represent
the Samaritan ethics associated with work, that is, ethics that
drives people to serve others without necessarily expecting
compensation[218].

Asceticism

Biblical goodness, as we defined it earlier on, is outward-
looking; it engages the world in an effort to promote justice,
beauty and ethics. It is simultaneously social and personal, for
in the pursuit of imbuing the world with these qualities, a person develops character and grows to be a good man or a good
woman. Asceticism is the opposite, it seeks withdrawal from
the world. Goodness enhances our humanity, asceticism sub-
tracts from it; goodness enhances our scope of action while asceticism restricts it with a long list of positive and negative
rules. Tertullian was a master at writing down such rules, especially negative ones, that is, things not to do.

In our contemporary society, ascetic attitudes have long
been left behind and our problem lies in the opposite direction,
that is, permissiveness. Asceticism may seem therefore a topic
of limited interest to us. But the systemic study of living systems, both biological and social, teaches us that life depends
upon a stable equilibrium and that a departure to either side,
either left or right, results in similar threats. That is, the impact
of such departures tends to be symmetrical. If we apply this to
our subject at hand, we can say that both asceticism and permissiveness produce similar threats to society and that peculi-
arities found in one are also found in the other.

We should therefore not dismiss Tertullian as one more
oddball in the history of the church but consider him seriously.

---

[217] Schaff, n.d.c., On Prayer, XXVIII
[218] For a detailed definition of Samaritan ethics, see J. D. R. de Raadt and
Veronica D. de Raadt, 2014.

He particularly aimed his asceticism at sexuality – also a very contemporary topic – and things related to it such as virginity and marriage. Mishandled human sexuality, whether it be permissive or ascetic, often conceives woman as a desirable object and man as its subject. For example, in modern society, commerce employs lightly clad women to sell almost anything to men. Asceticism also focuses on the desirability of woman, but in reverse, for as we have said, the effects of extremes upon society tend to be symmetrical. Thus Tertullian regarded women as "the devil's gateway" and bids them:

> ...go about in humble garb, and rather to affect meanness of appearance, walking about as Eve mourning and repentant, in order that by every garb of penitence she might the more fully expiate that which she derives from Eve, —the ignominy, I mean, of the first sin, and the odium (attaching to her as the cause) of human perdition... And do you not know that you are (each) an Eve? ...You are the devil's gateway: you are the unsealer of that (forbidden) tree: you are the first deserter of the divine law: you are she who persuaded him whom the devil was not valiant enough to attack. You destroyed so easily God's image, man.[219]

While Tertullian considered "the devil's gateway" as part of women's nature, modernity manipulates women to assume a similar role which ends up exploiting both women and men.

From here, Tertullian moved on to attack marriage. He did it by defining goodness in terms of various types of virginity and sexuality as something of a bane which one would desire to get rid of. For him,

> "virginity from one's birth... is (the virginity) of happiness, (and consists in) total ignorance of that from which you will afterwards wish to be freed...[220]

In his treatise "On Exhortation to Chastity" he brushed aside all sexual desires as "concupiscence", even the desire of a man

---

[219] Schaff, n.d.d., On the Apparel of Women, I, I
[220] Schaff, n.d.d., On Exhortation to Chastity, I

for his own wife. This in turn led him to conclude that, since marriage is the outcome of the spouses desiring each other, marriage itself "...consists of that which is the essence of fornication."[221] In another treatise "On Modesty" he opposed forgiveness of either adultery or fornication. He defended this by arguing that Paul had, "against his will", granted permission for people to marry only to avoid them engaging in fornication which he knew to be unforgivable. Had fornication or adultery been forgiveable, Paul, according to Tertullian, would have been bound to prohibit marriage[222]. It is difficult to see the consistency between these two treatises, but there can be no doubt that in both of them Tertullian showed a very poor regard of marriage. This dealt a severe blow on humanity, for marriage and family were the building blocks and overall model of a civilised society. They represented the necessary stable equilibrium for a community to preserve its humanity. His views were an attempt to thrust the community into a disequilibrium marked by asceticism. Conversely, modern attitudes to marriage and family are moving society towards a disequilibrium in the opposite direction, that is, permissiveness. Regardless of the direction, both are lethal.

Tertullian also wrote down moral prescriptions covering topics such as entertainment and dress. He rightly condemned "...public exhibition of charioteering frenzy, or gladiatorial gore, or scenic foulness...". But he failed to equip his people with the ability to discern between beneficial and detrimental participation in sports and drama and simply pours a blanket condemnation on all of these.

Orthodoxy

As we have said, Tertullian became somewhat disillusioned with developments in the church in mid-life. Up to then he had

---

[221] Schaff, n.d.d., On Exhortation to Chastity, IX. He supports this by misinterpreting Matthew 5:28; in this passage Jesus is speaking about adultery, that is, the situation of a man desiring a woman other than his wife or the wife of another man.
[222] Schaff, n.d.d., On Modesty, XVI

continued along the path of Ireneaus' rule of truth – he called it the "rule of faith" – although carried it to a further stage of orthodox rigidity. However, later in life, he was influenced by the teachings of the Montanist sect and exchanged the rule of faith for its "new prophecy". This became the guiding light of his thought and it led him to reject some of his earlier ideas. Although his rule of faith had a more lasting effect on the church than the new prophecy, the latter is of interest today because it shares many characteristics of the modern Charismatic movement. We will deal with his views on the rule of faith and new prophecy separately.

The Rule of Faith

In his usual legal manner, Tertullian set up prescriptions[223] to build an orthodox creed that must have contributed some of the material for what later became known as the *Apostle's Creed*. Apart from his extreme asceticism, he is best known for having been the first to introduce the term "Trinity"[224] into the theological vocabulary of the church. However, we need not concern ourselves with this; Tertullian's placing his rule of faith above Scripture as the sole authority of correct interpretation is of greater importance to our inquiry:

> Our appeal, therefore, must not be made to the Scriptures... For wherever it shall be manifest that the true Christian rule and faith shall be, there will likewise be the true Scriptures and expositions thereof, and all the Christian traditions.[225]

He left no space for theological debate outside the ambit of the rule of faith, especially when arguing against heretics. He believed that the rule of faith accurately represented the apostle's teaching and therefore he confidently closed the matter by bluntly stating '...our faith owes deference to the apostle, who forbids us to enter on "questions," or to lend our ears to new-

---

[223] Schaff, n.d.c., Anti-Marcion, I, XIII
[224] Schaff, n.d.c., Against Praxeas, XI
[225] Schaff, n.d.c., Anti-Marcion, I, XIX

fangled statements...'[226]. This may have avoided wasting time and effort through fighting against outlandish ideas that were cropping up in the church, for as any scholar knows, the most difficult and frustrating debate is against ignorance or lunacy. However, Tertullian assumed that the rule of faith accurately represented Christ's teaching and thus placed it beyond critical examination. Yet, the rule of faith was very much in need of critical examination. For, as I have repeatedly argued, expressions of biblical thought in the Hellenic language and their framework of thought were at best simplistic and failed to reflect the central historiological[227] thrust of Scripture. Just as detrimental was the intellectual wall that Tertullian built around the rule of faith. Like most of his predecessors, he excluded all disciplines other than theology from the inspiration of God's Spirit. Here again is the Greek tendency to freeze out the world it studies and to compartmentalise thought. These are opposed to the Hebrew integration of thought and observing the world in its full historical dynamic.

The New Prophecy

One effect of rigid orthodoxy is that, due to its static nature, after a period it fails to inspire many people's lives. They then seek variations to orthodoxy or other alternative beliefs. This happened towards the end of the second century when Montanus, in Asia Minor, led a movement that sought to revive the spirit of prophecy experienced during the apostolic era of the church. This movement claimed that the Holy Spirit had directly delivered to them a "new prophecy". This was received by Montanus while in a state of ecstasy somewhat parallel to the experiences of the modern charismatic movement. It is not clear to what degree Tertullian involved himself with this movement, but he certainly embraced the new prophecy and yielded to it the place previously held by the rule of faith.

---

[226] Schaff, n.d.c., Anti-Marcion, I, XVI

[227] By historiological I mean a form of reasoning, described by Ortega y Gasset, 2004, that assumes history to be driven by a constant nucleus. Biblical history is driven by the fall of man and by his and the Creation's redemption through Jesus Christ.

As a result of the new prophecy, Tertullian radically shifted from his strict legal manner of thinking to depending on prophecies delivered through a spiritual rapture. For him, what was received by such experiences transcended reasoning or understanding, citing Jesus' transfiguration[228] as an illustration:

> Now, it is no difficult matter to prove the rapture of Peter. For how could he have known Moses and Elias, except (by being) in the Spirit? People could not have had their images, or statues, or likenesses; for that the law forbade. How, if it were not that he had seen them in the Spirit? And therefore, because it was in the Spirit that he had now spoken, and not in his natural senses, he could not know what he had said.[229]

And, rather than the rule of faith, now the new prophecy became the rightful interpreter of Scripture:

> ...the Holy Ghost... has accordingly now dispersed all the perplexities of the past, and their self-chosen allegories and parables, by the open and perspicuous explanation of the entire mystery, through the new prophecy, which descends in copious streams from the Paraclete.[230]

Therefore, understanding of the Trinity was now given "...to every one who hears and receives the words of the new prophecy..."[231]. This meant that some teachings of the NT – referred to by him as the "new law" – were now superseded by the new prophecy. For example, while the NT permitted the remarriage of widows and widowers, this was now forbidden by the new prophecy. According to him:

> The New Law abrogated divorce—it had (somewhat) to abrogate; the New Prophecy (abrogates) second mar-

---

[228] Luke 9:29-33
[229] Schaff, n.d.c., Against Marcion, IV, XXII
[230] Schaff, n.d.c., On the Resurrection of the Flesh, LXIII
[231] Schaff, n.d.c., Against Praxeas, XXX

riage, (which is) no less a divorce of the former (marriage).[232]

Most perplexing is that he no longer supported the legitimacy of the institutional church but redefined it by distinguishing between spiritual and carnal persons whom he called "psychics":

> to the Psychics, since they receive not the Spirit, the things which are the Spirit's are not pleasing. Thus, so long as the things which are the Spirit's please them not, the things which are of the flesh will please, as being the contraries of the Spirit.[233]

All carnal people belonged to the grey area – the moat I defined earlier on – regardless of belonging to the clerical rank or the laity. The true church was represented only by spiritual people:

> ... accordingly "the Church,"... [will be]... the Church of the Spirit, by means of a spiritual man; not the Church which consists of a number of bishops. For the right and arbitrament is the Lord's, not the servant's; God's Himself, not the priest's.[234]

Yet these significant changes in Tertullian's teaching, which he claimed were inspired by the new prophecy, had no significant impact on the ongoing orthodoxy of the church. Far more influential were his treatises written within the scope of the rule of faith. His legally worded "prescriptions", including his introduction of the Trinity, had considerably more influence on the creeds that the church was to adopt later on.

Conclusions

Tertullian did not make significant alterations to what was already considered orthodox by the institutional church. His

---

[232] Schaff, n.d.d., On Monogamy, XIV
[233] Schaff, n.d.d., On Monogamy, I
[234] Schaff, n.d.d., On Modesty, XXI

mind was too bureaucratic and legal to be creative. But he certainly helped cement each of the socio-cultural factors under consideration, that was his immediate contribution (see Table 3). In the longer term his asceticism, especially his views on sexuality and marriage, although frowned upon by his contemporaries, left a lasting mark on the church. It strongly influenced the lives of the monastic orders; much later, even the more radical sectors within protestantism adopted his ascetic attitudes by frowning upon such things as dancing, playing cards and the theatre. On the positive side, his intellectual standing and his honesty provided yet one more link in the chain of reputable men who accepted the historical legitimacy of the events recorded in the NT.

8 Clement of Alexandria

One can discern two types of men among the Early Fathers. The first type was Eastern, true Hellenists with a decided theoretical and philosophical leaning. They were interested in searching for ultimate truths about life and the universe, a search that Tertullian would have certainly told them to abandon, since Christians had already embraced the "rule of faith" and in it they had all the knowledge they needed. Tertullian, together with Ignatius and Irenaeus, belonged to a second type of thinking; they represented the West and Rome and had a more organisational and practical turn of mind. By practical I mean that, rather than philosophising, they preferred to define with precepts how Christians ought to live and to set up the social structure to ensure they lived according to them. Yet, though the manner of thinking of these two types of Fathers diverged in many aspects, their ideas were blended together in order to shape the emerging church. The East provided the basis of knowledge and the West the model of bureaucratic administration through which the bishops and presbyters exercised control.

We have now reached a period where our survey must turn to the East. During this period – extending from the end of the second century and the beginning of the third – Alexandria was still the Hellenic and cultural capital of the world. In Alexandria there was a Christian Catechetical School[235] and two of its teachers were Clement and Origen. Together with Justin – although he was not from Alexandria – they represented the philosophical strand of the church that went on to introduce theology into Christianity. Although their focus of study remained the Scriptures, their thinking was heavily influenced by Plato, Philo and later on by Plotinus, the father of neo-platonism. Since Philo provided a method of studying the Bible, traces of which may be identified in Clement and especially

---

[235] It is not clear to what extent this was a formally organised school. But at least it was a school of thought made up of a group of scholars whose work coheres because of a common way of thinking.

Origen, we shall begin by looking at some of Philo's ideas on the matter.

Philo

Philo was a Hellenic-Jewish philosopher who lived from around 20 B.C to 50 A.D. He attempted to build a bridge between Plato and the OT and of particular significance was the way he harmonised the accounts of the Creation by Plato and the Bible. As we have said, the OT prophets regarded God's Creation of the world and its ongoing sustenance as all-important, for it was not only their habitat, but also the channel of communication of conveying God's speech to them. This speech provided meaning and guidance to people's life and work. We need not be surprised therefore, that Philo on encountering an account of the Creation by Plato – whom he evidently admired – would have shown a keen interest in its resemblance to Genesis. He went on to use Plato's ideas as a template to understand the OT and unwittingly, by doing this, he unfolded an intellectual quandary from which Christendom has not been able to extricate itself to this day. For beyond the similarities, there are some subtle yet profound differences between Plato and the OT. Should we overlook them, we will end up thinking in a manner that radically differs from the biblical prophets. This in turn will raise a significant obstacle to understanding what they wrote. Consider the following passage of Plato telling us that the world was fashioned after a perfect and eternal pattern – i.e. non-created:

> Now everything that becomes or is created must of necessity be created by some cause, for *without a cause nothing can be created*. The work of the creator, whenever he looks to the unchangeable and fashions the form and nature of his work after an *unchangeable pattern*, must necessarily be made fair and perfect... Which of the patterns had the artificer in view when he made the world – the pattern of the unchangeable, or of that which is created? If the world be indeed fair and the artificer good, it is manifest that he must have

looked to that which is eternal; but if what cannot be said without blasphemy is true, then to the created pattern. Every one will see that he must have looked to the eternal; for the world is the fairest of creations and he is the best of causes.[236]

What Plato really described in this passage was not the *creation* of the world, but its *production*[237]. Creation, at least in the biblical sense, meant pure design, something completely new, created out of nothing. But such an idea was foreign to Plato; for him there had to be an initial "cause" and this, he told us, was an "eternal" and "unchangeable pattern", it was a sort of fixed model[238]. In addition, this pattern was not only important to explain the origin of the world, but it was also the fountain of true reason:

> That which is apprehended by *intelligence and reason is always in the same state*; but that which is conceived by opinion with the help of sensation and without reason, is always in a process of becoming and perishing and *never really is.*[239]

In other words, this "unchangeable pattern" was the only reality and the only realm where intelligent thinking could take place. Outside it, people were left only with opinions and sensations that had no constancy and were of limited worth to wisdom and science. This was not only Plato's view, but the view of other Greek thinkers as well, even if they expressed it in different words. We will refer to this thinking as *dialectical reasoning*[240].

---

[236] Plato, 2008, emphasis added

[237] The ancient Greek language did not have a verb equivalent to the Hebrew *bara* (H1254) commonly translated as *create*; the closest to this was *poieo* (G 4160) which is used in the NT. It means to make something out of something, not out of nothing.

[238] The Greek term for this was *eidos*, often translated into English as *form*.

[239] Plato, 2008, emphasis added

[240] Ortega y Gasset, 2004, VIII, calls it "physico-mathematical" reason to describe what is practised in modernity. But since its origin is far more ancient, I prefer to call it *dialectical thinking* to reflect its Greek origin.

On the other hand, the prophets knew of no unchangeable pattern used by God to create the world. According to them, God created the world out of nothing by personally issuing his commands. These commands were not only spoken at the beginning of time but were continuously delivered through his Spirit in order to sustain the Creation. God's commands were the proper focus of a prophet's reasoning and were communicated to the people through his Spirit in the law, the prophets and in the Creation itself. God spoke and everything happened accordingly[241]. Therefore, to be able to reason, they had to listen first to his commands, either spoken or delivered uninterruptedly – day and night[242] – through the Creation. That is, the prophet's reasoning was always based on empirical events witnessed by either listening to God's voice or by observing his activity in the world. This was the basis of their historical reasoning[243].

This meant that Plato had effectively erected two barriers before God. The first, the "unchangeable pattern", he placed between God and the world. The second was an epistemological barrier: no thought, except pure reason, could reach the truth. Empirical reality, so important to the prophet who received it as God's speech, was not real to Plato. Philo allowed these barriers to be imposed not only upon himself but also upon Moses:

> Moses... was well aware that it is indispensable that in all existing things there must be an *active cause*, and a passive subject; and that *the active cause is the intellect of the universe*, thoroughly unadulterated and thor-

---

[241] Psalm 33:9

[242] Psalm 19:2

[243] As termed by Ortega y Gasset, 2004, VIII. For a discussion of historical reasoning, see J. D. R. de Raadt, 2013, p. 50-57. Interestingly, the word history is of Greek origin (historía) and according to Aristóteles it signified "an account of one's inquiries", MLSJ. That is, history is about something observed rather based on pure dialectical reason. Therefore, the expression *natural history* is commonly used to represent the study of plants and animals based on observation rather than on the standard methodology of the natural sciences.

oughly unmixed, superior to virtue and superior to science, superior even to abstract good or abstract beauty;
while the passive subject is something inanimate and
incapable of motion by any intrinsic power of its own,
but *having been set in motion, and fashioned, and endowed with life by the intellect, became transformed
into that most perfect work, this world.*[244]

Philo, having accepted the Platonic barrier between God and
his Creation, which elsewhere he described as "the archetypal
model, the idea of ideas, the Reason [Logos] of God"[245], asser-
ted that this model was comprehensible "only [to] the very
purest intellect."[246] And by the "purest intellect" Philo meant
the dialectical reasoning of the Greek philosophers. With one
stroke he wiped away the historical reasoning of the prophets
and the ability to make sense of passages of the OT that were
difficult, if not impossible, to understand through dialectical
reasoning. Passages that did not lend themselves to dialectical
interpretation should be treated as allegories.

An example of this is Genesis 4:17. This verse states that
Cain built a city. Philo questioned whether it was possible for
Cain to build a city and resolved the problem by interpreting
the verse as an allegory:

> And it may become us next to consider on what ac-
> count this same man [Cain] is represented as founding
> and building a city, for it is only a multitude of men
> who have need of a city to dwell in... And moreover,
> besides all these things, would he be able to carry bur-
> dens, to move away masses of earth, to widen narrow
> passages, to make fountains and water-courses, and all
> the other things with which a city ought to be
> provided? Perhaps, therefore, since all these ideas are
> inconsistent with truth, it would be better to look upon
> the statement as an allegory, and to say that Cain de-
> termined to build up his own doctrine like a city.[247]

---

[244] Philo, 1993, On the Creation II, 8
[245] Philo, 1993, On the Creation, VI, 25
[246] Philo, 1993, The Special Laws, I, 46
[247] Philo, 1993, On the Posterity of Cain and His Exile, XIV, 49-51

The Hebrew word that is translated into English as "city" is *yir* (H5892); it can mean city, but it also can mean "encampment or post" or "a permanent settlement without reference to size or claims."[248] Therefore, there is no need to question the accuracy of this verse. Granted, given the time in which Philo lived he can be excused for lacking the knowledge of ancient languages we have available today. But he jumped to conclusions far too early and by doing so, set a dangerous precedent for the allegorical interpretation of Scripture. This method of interpretation gave license to reading anything one wished to in a text. In the passage just cited, Philo presumed "city" to stand for "doctrine" without providing any rationale for this. And this is the perennial problem that pure rationalism ultimately generates, whether it be espoused by Greek philosophy or by modernity: it dissolves into irrationally[249].

Having made such critical remarks against Greek rationality, one ought not to undervalue the common metaphysical insight that Plato, Philo and other philosophers had regarding the world. They shared with the OT the conviction that, behind our observed world, especially when one considered its beauty and the amazing workings of nature, there stood a Providence, regardless of whether or not they understood Providence in a personal or impersonal manner. This awareness, Paul argued, was revealed by the hand of God himself[250] and received by them through faith. Plato, Aristotle and others would have agreed with this[251]. But we must now leave this matter and return to Alexandria and the Early Fathers who taught there.

Clement

Of the two Alexandrian scholars, Origin is the most highly regarded, perhaps because he is understood to be the first sys-

---

[248] TWOT, 1615

[249] For example, the rationalism that once more raised its head in the 17th century – e.g. Spinoza and Descartes – eventually gave way to Nietzsche's nihilism and led to our contemporary irrational post-modernity.

[250] Romans 1:19-20

[251] Schaff, n.d.b., The Stromata, II, IV

tematic theologian. This is significant for the clergy but from the laity's point of view, Clement is far more important. For Clement, among the Early Fathers, was one who came the closest to the biblical idea of man, his science, his place in society and his work. Seen in this light, he was above any of the Early Fathers, with the possible exception of Augustine. Undeniably, he was somewhat influenced by the dialectical rationalism of Plato and Philo. Yet, he seemed to have had more common sense than the rest of the fathers. He seemed to have perceived the down-to-earth nature of Scripture; using philosophy and the arts in subservience to it, he was able to make significant advances in Christian thought. Indeed, he anticipated the humanists of the 16th Century, especially Erasmus, Vives, Melanchthon and Calvin[252]. His writings cover subjects such as the relationship between faith and reason and the importance of work and the arts that, more than a millennium later, would play a major role in the Christian Renascence. Let us begin by considering the foundation of his thinking.

The Logos

There is an intriguing passage in Philo's writings stating that:

> the Father of the universe has caused him [Logos] to spring up as the eldest son, whom, in another passage, he [Moses] calls the firstborn; and he who is thus born, imitating the ways of his father, has formed such and such species, looking to his archetypal patterns.[253]

No one has been able to establish with certainty the extent to which Philo influenced John or Paul's[254] writings. Yet, the passage above provides some evidence that the perception of a Son of God was floating about at the time of Christ, even among non Christian philosophers such as Philo. When Clem-

[252] For a discussion of these humanists see de J. D. R. Raadt, 2013, p. 65-74.
[253] Philo, 1993, On the Confusion of Tongues, XIV, 63
[254] Colossians 1:15-18

ent came across this insight, he concluded that philosophers also "hear[d] God's voice while closely contemplating the fabric of the universe..."[255]. This meant that their philosophy could be useful for the study of Scripture.

The apostles, however, never depersonalised the Logos. Having met Jesus in the flesh, it would have been clearly absurd to think of him as some incarnate intellectual rationality. But the Early Fathers had no such experience and were therefore more susceptible to accept a Platonic interpretation. As we saw earlier, Justin was the first to speculate that the Logos was a rational principle governing the universe. Clement also shows a trace of this influence. He believed that the Word of God was "intellectual" and that science should govern human affairs by focusing on "the archetypes above"[256], that is, Plato's perfect models. But he was not entirely dominated by rationalism when dealing with other important subjects such as philosophy, the arts and work. Here, he made a remarkable humanistic contribution, for he perceived that the breadth and depth of the Logos spanned everything:

> Suffice it for me to say, that the Lord of all is God; and I say the Lord of all absolutely, nothing being left by way of exception.[257]

His perception widened the vision of the church beyond the narrow scope of theological matters and ascetic morality. He saw the momentous pedagogical agenda of Christ, witnessed not only in the Scriptures, but also by the philosophers who, like Plato, had heard his voice. It led him to praise him by exclaiming "Well done, Plato! Thou hast touched on the truth. But do not flag. Undertake with me the inquiry respecting the Good."[258] And inquiry about "the Good" ought to start with the knowledge of self:

---

[255] Schaff, n.d.b., The Stromata, V, XIV
[256] Schaff, n.d.b., The Stromata, VI, IX
[257] Schaff, n.d.b., The Stromata, VI, XVII
[258] Schaff, n.d.b., Exhortation to the Heathen, VI

> The expression, "Know thyself,"...may be an injunction
> to the pursuit of knowledge. For it is not possible to
> know the parts without the essence of the whole; and
> one must study the genesis of the universe, that thereby
> we may be able to learn the nature of man.[259]

Clement's understanding of goodness was not some narrow asceticism; on the contrary, it took in the entire breadth of the
universe. Goodness was not attained by obeying a long list of
precepts of things not to be done, but by knowing oneself. Self
knowledge had, since ancient times, been acknowledged as the
heart of education. And together with this injunction Clement
laid down some principles necessary to fulfil it. One had to
start one's inquiry by grasping the totality and then move on to
the parts. Moreover, knowing self went together with knowing
God, without knowledge of whom there could no understanding of ourselves[260].

Next, Clement considered faith had to precede understanding no matter what approach one took to thinking:

> Should one say that Knowledge is founded on demon-
> stration by a process of reasoning, let him hear that first
> principles are incapable of demonstration; for they are
> known neither by art nor sagacity... Hence it is thought
> that the first cause of the universe can be apprehended
> by faith alone.[261]

Clement claimed Aristotle agreed with this[262]. But, for Clement, the dependence of knowledge on faith was reciprocal.
Learning demanded faith, but faith also required learning. He
had no sympathy for anti-intellectual attitudes:

> Some, who think themselves naturally gifted, do not
> wish to touch either philosophy or logic; nay more,
> they do not wish to learn natural science. They demand
> bare faith alone, as if they wished, without bestowing

[259] Schaff, n.d.b., The Stromata, I, XIV
[260] Schaff, n.d.b., The Instructor, III, I
[261] Schaff, n.d.b., The Stromata, II, IV
[262] Schaff, n.d.b., The Stromata, II, IV

> any care on the vine, straightway to gather clusters from the first... So also here, I call him truly learned who brings everything to bear on the truth; so that, from geometry, and music, and grammar, and philosophy itself, culling what is useful, he guards the faith against assault.[263]

The writer of the book of Hebrews defined faith as the substance of the things biblical people hoped for[264], the vision of a world for which they yearned. Without this sort of vision they would have perished. They may have survived biologically, but their spirit would have died. They would have died by pursuing the wrong vision or by having no vision at all. Or, although having a vision, they could have been crushed by believing that learning was unnecessary to attain it. They could not have the will to undergo the discipline that learning demanded, for:

> ...volition takes the precedence of all; for the intellectual powers are ministers of the Will. "Will," it is said, "and thou shalt be able."[265]

This is most relevant. Sceptics seldom understand that their disbelief is not based on them being unable to accept some event – such as Christ's resurrection – as truthful, but rather the outcome of them being unwilling to believe right from the beginning. Their unwillingness leads them to collect some fragmented evidence that in their opinion justifies their disbelief. But belief must start with the will to believe in order to capture the totality, or as Clement said above, grasp "the essence of the whole". Only then one can understand the parts and judge whether the events once held as objections to believing are truly valid.

---

[263] Schaff, n.d.b., The Stromata, I, IX
[264] Hebrews, 11:1
[265] Schaff, n.d.b., The Stromata, II, XVII

Education and the Arts

Let us consider what sort of learning is required by faith. Clement listed geometry, music, grammar and philosophy among the disciplines mastered by an educated person. He attributed "all this artistic and skilful invention" to God[266]. Yet he warned that it should be not received indiscriminately, but that it should be sieved in order to obtain what was useful. Such culling was necessary because much of the arts and philosophy came via Hellenism[267], which meant that not all could be accepted indiscriminately. Nevertheless, he recognised the immense cultural contribution furnished by the Greek people, something he did not regard as accidental but, on the contrary, a gift from the hand of God:

> The Greek preparatory culture, therefore, with philosophy itself, is shown to have come down from God to men, not with a definite direction but in the way in which showers fall down on the good land, and on the dunghill, and on the houses.[268]

Anticipating anti-intellectual arguments built on Paul's warning against philosophy, Clement stated that Paul did not outrightly reject philosophy, but only disapproved the false philosophy taught by Epicureans and Stoics[269]. He set the following criterion to separate the philosophical wheat from the chaff:

> [good] philosophy is characterised by investigation into truth and the nature of things (this is the truth of which the Lord Himself said, "I am the truth" [John xiv. 6]); and that [truth] *exercises the mind, rouses the intelligence, and begets an inquiring shrewdness...*[270]

---

[266] Schaff, n.d.b., The Stromata, I, IV
[267] I say *came via* and not *originated with* because Clement believed that much of philosophy was derived from people who were not Greeks, but included Israel's prophets. For example, "Plato the philosopher, [was] aided in legislation by the books of Moses..." (Schaff, n.d.b., The Stromata, I, XV; I, XXV).
[268] Schaff, n.d.b., The Stromata, I, VII
[269] Schaff, n.d.b., The Stromata, I, XI
[270] Schaff, n.d.b., The Stromata, I, V

People who pursued such truth as this would have stood in sharp contrast to the malleable and dependent behaviour encouraged by Ignatius or Tertullian; they were the people who would have turned the world upside down.

Just as there was a reciprocal relationship between faith and learning, there was the same link between philosophy and Scripture. Philosophy aided the search for Biblical truth, but Biblical truth established the criterion for good philosophy[271]. Such philosophising was "necessary... for him who desires to be partaker of the power of God..."[272], that is, for a mature and educated Christian. It was a radical departure from the conception of Christian perfection due to mysticism and ethereal spirituality.   Clement redefined philosophy. Greek philosophy sought after ultimate truth about knowledge (epistemology) and reality (ontology). It was a theoretical endeavour that elevated thought above everyday life, especially dysfunctional life. For Clement, philosophy was systemic understanding of the whole, based on the integration of all disciplines:

> And philosophy—I do not mean the Stoic, or the Platonic, or the Epicurean, or the Aristotelian, but whatever has been well said by each of those sects, which teach righteousness along with a science pervaded by piety, – *this eclectic whole I call philosophy*.[273]

And by a righteous and pious life he did not mean a monastic life but one lived in the real world, engaged in family, society and work. We turn to this in the next section.

---

[271] Such was the closeness Clement saw between Scripture and philosophy, that he believed there was a Hebrew philosophy that preceded the Greek by many generations. See Schaff, n.d.b., The Stromata, I, XIX.

[272] Schaff, n.d.b., The Stromata, I, IX

[273] Schaff, n.d.b., The Stromata, I, VII, emphasis added. Clement's definition of philosophy anticipates Erasmus' Philosophy of Christ and even 20th century general system theory described as the "skeleton of science", Boulding, 1956.

Society, Family and Work

Like some of his predecessors, Clement differentiated between a lukewarm and an exemplary Christian. His definition of the exemplary person was "the Gnostic [i.e. the truly wise] who is after the image and likeness of God, who imitates God as far as possible..."[274]. An exemplary life was not attained through ecstatic experiences, raptures of the Spirit or by practising asceticism. On the contrary, Clement rejected asceticism that led to pain or poverty, for he considered the privation of the normal needs of the body detrimental to a Christian's closeness to God[275]. Instead, he advocated moderation:

> Our mode of life is not to accustom us to voluptuousness and licentiousness, nor to the opposite extreme, but to the medium between these, that which is harmonious and temperate, and free of either evil, luxury and parsimony.[276]

Nor did he assume the clergy to be gnostic by default. On the contrary, he viewed gnostics as comprising a "true" non-institutional "clergy":

> Those... who have exercised themselves in the Lord's commandments, and lived perfectly and gnostically according to the Gospel, may be enrolled in the chosen body of the apostles. Such a one is in reality a presbyter of the Church, and a true minister (deacon) of the will of God, if he do[es] and teach what is the Lord's; not as being ordained by men, nor regarded righteous because a presbyter, but enrolled in the presbyterate because righteous.[277]

---

[274] Schaff, n.d.b., The Stromata, II, XIX. Although the word *gnostic* – which literally meant in possession of knowledge – was used at the time to identify the followers of gnosticism, Clement wrestled the word away from them to apply it to the people he truly regarded as wise and knowledgeable.

[275] Schaff, n.d.b., The Stromata, IV, V

[276] Schaff, n.d.b., The Instructor, III, X

[277] Schaff, n.d.b., The Stromata, VI, XIII

It is surprising that such a challenging statement did not rouse a protest from the clerical hierarchy of that day. For this passage, although not openly rejecting the existing leadership of the church, set above it another group of people. It comprised members of the laity who had become "noble and good not by nature, but by learning"[278] and who sought "the truth [and the kingdom of heaven] in word and deed..."[279].

Clement rejected individualism and embraced a "socialistic"[280] view of the kingdom of heaven. He believed that there were limits to personal wealth and property dictated by the needs of the community as a whole and by a spirit of sharing what was ultimately God's property:

> God brought our race into communion by first imparting what was His own, when He gave His own Word, common to all, and made all things for all. All things therefore are common, and not for the rich to appropriate an undue share. That expression, therefore, "I possess, and possess in abundance: why then should I not enjoy?" is suitable neither to the man, nor to society. But more worthy of love is that: "I have: why should I not give to those who need?" For such a one—one who fulfils the command, "Thou shalt love thy neighbour as thyself"—is perfect. For this is the true luxury—the treasured wealth. But that which is squandered on foolish lusts is to be reckoned waste, not expenditure. For God has given to us, I know well, the liberty of use, but only so far as necessary; and He has determined that the use should be common. And it is monstrous for one to live in luxury, while many are in want. How much more glorious is it to do good to many, than to live sumptuously! How much wiser to spend money on human beings, than on jewels and gold! How much more

---

[278] Schaff, n.d.b., The Stromata, I, VI. The order of the words in the original has been rearranged.

[279] Schaff, n.d.b., The Stromata, IV, V

[280] A term used by Kuyper (1950, p. 41) at The Netherlands' First Christian Social Congress in1891 to describe a social vision that closely approximated Clement's views.

useful to acquire decorous friends, than lifeless orna-
ments![281]

In this sort of society marriage and family occupied a high
place. Clement regarded the family as a pivotal point of the
Creation and a model of social structure, where humanity is a
family and God the father of all:

> It becomes us who truly follow the Scripture to enjoy
> ourselves temperately, as in Paradise. We must regard
> the woman's crown to be her husband, and the hus-
> band's crown to be marriage; and the flowers of mar-
> riage the children of both, which the divine husband-
> man plucks from meadows of flesh. "Children's chil-
> dren are the crown of old men." [Proverbs 17:6] And
> the glory of children is their fathers, it is said; and our
> glory is the Father of all; and the crown of the whole
> church is Christ.[282]

Within this model society, Clement provided us with a work
ethic for both men and women that was chiefly centred around
the family. It must not be forgotten that in the ancient world,
the centre of the economy was the household. Clement regarded it as "no disgrace..."[283] for both men and women to engage in the physical work necessary to sustain their families.
On the contrary, he discouraged employing servants, especially
in large numbers. He lamented the employment of "herds of
beautiful boys, like cattle, from whom they [their masters]
milk away their beauty."[284]

Finally, he ascribed the same worth to intellectual and physical work. He rejected anti-intellectualism as much as the disdain for manual work:

> Accordingly[,] discourse refreshes the soul and entices
> it to nobleness; and happy is he who has the use of both
> his hands. Neither, therefore, is he who can act well to

---

[281] Schaff, n.d.b., The Instructor, II, XIII
[282] Schaff, n.d.b., The Instructor, II, VIII
[283] Schaff, n.d.b., The Instructor, III, X
[284] Schaff, n.d.b., The Instructor, III, IV

be vilified by him who is able to speak well; nor is he who is able to speak well to be disparaged by him who is capable of acting well. But let each do that for which he is naturally fitted. What the one exhibits as actually done, the other speaks, preparing, as it were, the way for well-doing, and leading the hearers to the practice of good.[285]

Conclusion

Certainly Clement shines amongst the Early Fathers and church historians are unjust not to grant him the place of prominence he deserves. His work went against the Hellenic flow of the other Early Fathers and he reintroduced a biblical perspective into each of the social factors we have been considering (see Table 3-1). A large part of Clement's writings were echoed in the writings of the 16th century humanists associated with Erasmus. Yet, it would be incorrect to regard him as being ahead of his times. The opposite is closer to the truth. Erasmus and his followers had to travel back in time to retrieve the wisdom that lay buried for centuries in Clement's writings. That is why Erasmus' period of history is appropriately referred to as Renascence and, in particular, in the North of Europe as Christian Renascence. For it was the rebirth of the cultural and intellectual treasures of antiquity that had been buried during the Dark Ages. Among these treasures we should include Clement's work. Were it not for that recalcitrant element in man that leads him to frustrate the opportunities that are set in front of him, all the advances of the 17th century attained in Northern Europe could have blossomed following Clement's time. He already provided the intellectual foundation that ushered in the Renascence. Not only would Northern Europe have benefited, but the whole of Europe, and from there, science, the fine arts, technology and social welfare could have been disseminated to other continents. History could have been vastly different.

---

[285] Schaff, n.d.b., The Stromata, I, X

It may be worthwhile at this stage to ponder why this did not happen by reflecting on Jesus' parable of the talents[286]. In this parable, the first two servants were praised for having put their talents to work and multiplied what their master entrusted to them. Yet the focus of the story is the third servant and the character Jesus gave him. He could have been a rebel who told his master to keep his talent and put it to work himself. Or, he could have been a libertine who spent his talent on wine, women and song. Normally, rebels and libertines are a minority in society and of whom people disapprove. The third servant is neither a rebel nor a libertine. Jesus must have chosen this type because they represent a majority in society and their weakness – fear – is subtlety and easily disguised.

Fear was the engine behind the rise of the church's theology and bureaucracy. A rigid rule of faith was erected to protect people from falling into heresy. And an equally rigid ecclesiastical organisation was set up to ensure people did not become rebels or libertines. Yet, these measures robbed people of the very freedom that Jesus had come to institute. Jesus was not particularly worried about rebels and libertines; many became his followers and he regarded them as his friends[287] and saw them – publicans and harlots – leading the way to the kingdom of God[288]. His concern was fearful characters. They are the proverbial spanner in the works of history; their fear enslaves them. Soon after their release from Egypt, fear drove the Israelites to wish to forfeit their freedom in exchange for security, even if it meant returning to bondage. The outcome, we know, was forty years wandering in the wilderness.

Clement valued freedom and sought the truth that delivers it. Rather than setting up theological rules and imposing a clerical hierarchy over the people, he sought to equip them with the intellectual tools that came from the hand of God. For, with the help of philosophy and the arts, and by exerting himself in the study of Scripture, the wise man in Christ finds true

---

[286] Matthew 25:14-30
[287] Matthew 11:19, Mark 2:15-16
[288] Matthew 21:31

freedom. Clement was the Joshua and Caleb of his time whose enthusiasm for learning was brushed aside in the years that followed and resulted in Christendom wandering in the wilderness of the Dark Ages.

9 Neo-Platonism

Introduction

Since ancient times people have been puzzled by a paradox; on the one hand, their lives are contained within a universe which they experience as a closed system. This means they cannot – either physically or intellectually – go past its boundaries because the nature of a closed system is culturally suffocating and oppressive. At the same time, however, they observe many things and events within the universe that do not fit their conception of a closed system. These observations insistently point to something beyond the horizon – something that satisfies peoples' yearning. Indeed, most cultures have developed some conception of what lies beyond the horizon. Historically people have always sought to open a window to seek God or gods who might release them from the oppression they encounter. One instrument for their search is religion, a ritual of ceremonial practices and mysticism that might help to cross the boundaries of the universe and ascend to God. However, religion often disappoints; it leads to people living split lives that are difficult to connect with each other; one life is outside the world, the other inside.

At the time we are considering – the first half of the third century – people became disenchanted with religion in general and, in particular, the pure rationality of classical philosophy[289] as represented by Plato and Aristotle. Out of this disenchantment neo-platonism arose, a blend of classical philosophy and religion. It sought to fill the need of man to transcend the closed reality of life and ascend to what lay behind it. Its name, neo-platonism, is derived from its use of Plato's ideas but with a different purpose. Plato differentiated between the imperfect world in which we live and the perfect model from which it originated. He placed reason as part of the perfect model but applied it to understanding the imperfect world. Neo-platonism followed Plato in placing reason in the perfect

---

[289] See Tillich, 1968

model but, instead of applying it for understanding the imperfect world, it sought to understand the god who had used the perfect model to produce the world. It thus opened the door for philosophy to enter a domain that had so far mostly been the province of religion. Rather than providing a religious ritual, it offered a conceptual approach – albeit, purely speculative – to step outside the boundaries of the universe and to contemplate its god, "the One". In other words, it became a theology.

The home of neo-platonism was Alexandria and it was there where it greatly influenced Christian theology, not only in its content, but also its disciplinary method of discoursing about God. The major person to import neo-platonism into Christianity was carried out by Origen, a student of Clement and his successor as the head of the catechetical school of Alexandria. Origen was a contemporary of Plotinus, one of the main exponents of neo-platonism and it is possible that they both studied under the same teacher, Ammonius Saccas. Ammonius was an Alexandrian philosopher and one of the founders of neo-platonism. In the midst of this intellectual circle, Origen eagerly absorbed the speculative methods of neo-platonism and applied them to his study of Scriptures. In pursuit of this endeavour, he became the first Christian "systematic theologian"[290].

Moreover, beginning with Origen, Christian thought became almost fully identified with theology. Its contribution to philosophy and to the sciences in general was largely ignored. Whatever was gained from Clement in order to build a biblically-based philosophy, was lost with Origen. With him, significant elements of neo-platonic theology firmly wedged themselves in Christian theology displacing the corresponding biblical ideas. Most of these theological elements Origen borrowed from Plotinus and therefore we will start examining some of his ideas.

---

[290] Moore, n.d.; Kerr, 1966, p. 42

Plotinus

To understand Plotinus it is best to begin by considering what he thought about reality. He believed that there were two realities, which he respectively called Being and Non-Being (both beginning with capitals letters). He defined Being as follows:

> There exists a genuinely universal (Being). The world that we see is no more than its image. This veritably universal (Being) is in nothing; for nothing has proceeded from its existence... Do not therefore place our world in this genuinely universal (Being) as in a place, if by place you understand the limit of the body... Conceive their relation [between Being and place] *exclusively by the mind*, setting aside all local nomenclature. ...the universal (Being)... has no need of being in a place, nor in anything whatever. Being universal, it could not fail to support itself, for it fills itself, equals itself, and is where is the universal because it is this itself.[291]

For Plotinus, Being represented the only true reality, completely self contained and independent of everything else. However, Being was purely conceptual – something to be experienced only through man's intellect; it constituted what he called an "intelligible world".

In this world Plotinus placed his own trinity, but rather than being comprised of persons, it was formed by three principles: the One (also known as the Good), the universal Intelligence and the universal Soul. The highest principle was the Good and he defined it as follows:

> The Good is the principle on which all depends, to which everything aspires, from which everything issues, and of which everything has need. As to Him, *He suffices to himself*, being complete, so He stands in need of nothing; He is the measure and the end of all

---

[291] Plotinus, 2013b, VI, 4, 2; emphasis added

things; and *from Him spring intelligence*, being, soul, life, and intellectual contemplation.[292]

Rather than conceiving goodness as a quality possessed by something – such as a good meal or a good friend – Plotinus regarded the Good as a thing in itself and above all other things. And from this Good, said Plotinus, flows universal Intelligence, the second principle, an intelligence that was different to man's ordinary intelligence. He wrote:

> Intelligence itself... [is very different]... from what we call human intelligences. The latter indeed are all occupied with propositions, discussions about the meanings of words, reasonings, examinations of the validity of conclusions, observing the concatenation of causes, being incapable of possessing truth "a priori,"... Such is not the primary [universal] Intelligence. Though remaining within itself, it is all things; it possesses all things, without possessing them (in the usual acceptation of that term); the things that subsist in it not differing from it, and not being separated from each other. Each one of them is all the others, is everything and everywhere, although not confounded with other things, and remaining distinct therefrom.[293]

While the passage above makes it clear what human intelligence is, we are very much left in the dark regarding universal Intelligence. But then, this should not surprise us if we are trying to understand with our human intelligence something which Plotinus himself states is beyond it. It requires, according to Plotinus, "a superior manner" of reasoning. So we shall let the matter rest there for the moment but will only note that, according to Plotinus, from such universal Intelligence proceeded the universal Soul. We shall deal with this later when we examine man's soul.

Next we address Plotinus and the problem of evil. Evil or sin represented a point of convergence between the Bible and Greek moral philosophy, especially as espoused by Plato and

---

[292] Plotinus, 2013d, I, 8, 2; emphasis added
[293] Plotinus, 2013d, I, 8, 2

later Plotinus. Moral philosophers were as much aware and concerned about the evil among the people with which they lived as were the biblical prophets. One must admire these prophets and philosophers for their stand against evil for, throughout history, most societies and especially the elites that controlled them have regularly turned a blind eye on evil, except of course, when it concerned their own vested interests. We should not be surprised therefore, that given their common fight against evil, the Early Fathers should have woven together Greek philosophy and Hebrew prophecy. The theology that emerged from it, despite its many faults, provided for centuries a basis for morality and civility in Christendom. Much of the social ills of modernity can be explained by its having abandoned them.

But we must return to Plotinus. He argued that just as Being was ruled by the Good and since evil could not be placed in the intelligible world, there had to be a counterpart to Being, that is, another reality – where it belonged. This reality was Non-Being. Although the term seems equivalent to *non-reality*, he nevertheless insisted that non-reality existed, but thought it was only an image of Being "...or something still more distant from reality"[294]. Having found a place for evil, he went on to define it by contrasting it with good. In Table 9-1 I have tabulated four of these differences (the first four) and also listed some other qualities of evil that Plotinus added. He wrote that these "...are not the mere accidents of evil, but its very essence; all of that can be discovered when any part of evil is examined."[295]

It is a list of rather abstract categories, yet typical of his thought. It is an example of the lesser effectiveness of Greek philosophy when endeavouring to put its teachings into practice. And given that the society that surrounded Plotinus was marked by its gross lack of ethics, a more practical approach was much needed. The prophets had a different approach; they pointed to actual events that were evil – such as Nathan con-

---

[294] Plotinus, 2013d, I, 8, 3
[295] Plotinus, 2013d, I, 8, 3

demning David for taking Bathsheba1 – thereby exposing common attitudes among the people which they could readily identify within themselves and in others around them.

Table 9-1

Evil	Good
not measurable	measurable
indeterminate	determinate
unshaped	providing shape
wanting, inadequate	self-sufficient
without boundaries	
changeable	
passive	
insatiable	
absolutely poor	

When dealing with Plotinus, this difference of approach – abstract versus practical – may be explained by his belief that evil did not originate in people but in matter. Just as evil was non-reality, so matter was *non-entity*:

> ...matter is neither intelligence, nor life, nor ("seminal") reason, nor limit. It is a kind of infinity. Neither is it an (active) power; for what could it produce? Since matter is none of the above-mentioned things, it could not be called existence. It deserves only the name "nonentity" yet not even in the sense in which we may say that movement or rest are not existence; *matter is real non-entity.*[296]

Once he had established the universal Soul on the one hand and evil matter on the other, he was able to explain the origin of the "sense-world", the world people and the Bible called the

---

[296] Plotinus, 2013b, III, 6, 7

Creation. The sense-world was like an image of itself that the universal Soul had imprinted on matter. Albeit in a rather mundane manner, one can imagine this sense-world as the digital photograph that people take of themselves in our day and which they call a "selfie". Just as the digital image is not real, but only a resemblance – so Plotinus regarded the sense-world as a semi-real resemblance. It was only an approximation of the universal Soul and an intermediate state between Being and Non-Being, a combination of good – stemming from the universal Soul – and evil provided by matter. It resulted in the mix of good and evil observed in the world in which people lived. And the blame was laid on matter, which contrasted with the Bible which saw evil as originating in the inner man, in his heart[297].

In order to release man from this evil, Plotinus thought it necessary to separate man's soul from his body, just as Plato had done earlier. He regarded man's soul as belonging to part of the universal Soul. While it remained with the universal Soul, man's soul lived in a state of blessedness free from the cares of the sense-world. But when it separated itself from the universal soul and took upon himself flesh and blood – matter – it lost its privilege and experienced the hardships of life in the sense-world:

> Now when a [human] soul... withdraws from the universal Soul, and distinguishes herself therefrom... then, isolating herself in her individual existence, she weakens, and finds herself overwhelmed with a crowd of cares...[298]

Here we have Plotinus' version of the fall of man. Though differing from the biblical account, there was nevertheless a

---

[297] Proverbs 4:23; 'in its abstract meaning, "heart" became the richest biblical term for the totality of man's inner or immaterial nature. In biblical literature it is the most frequently used term for man's immaterial personality functions as well as the most inclusive term for them since, in the Bible, virtually every immaterial function of man is attributed to the "heart."' TWOT.
[298] Plotinus, 2013a, IV, 8, 4

resemblance between them as regards the human motive behind the fall as well as its consequences. This resemblance was
found in passages such as this:

> How does it happen that souls forget their paternal di-
> vinity? ...The origin of their evil is "audacity," ... and
> the desire to belong to none but themselves. As soon as
> they have enjoyed the pleasure of an independent life...
> they have arrived at such an "apostasy" (distance) from
> the Divinity, that they are even ignorant that they derive
> their life from Him....[299]

Such "audacity" of the soul wishing to become independent
was not too different to Eve's audacity of wanting to be like
God[300] and independent. The outcome in both cases was a life
of misery.

How could man be redeemed from such a predicament?
Here Plotinus and the Bible took different paths due to their
dissimilar conceptions of evil. The Bible saw man's sin as an
act of transgressing the law of God. It therefore dealt with it
juridically. Man was found guilty not because he *was* dishonest, but because he had *behaved* dishonestly. *Dishonesty* – an
adjective – was attributed to a person after *acting dishonestly* –
an adverb – and not the other way around. The guilt from this
action could only be removed by an *act* of retribution. In the
OT this retribution was rendered by a sacrifice at the altar. In
the NT, it was provided by the death of Christ.

Plotinus, on the other hand, saw evil as an attribute residing
in matter; matter *did* no evil, but *was* evil. Rather than a juridical redemption, Plotinus said that man needed to divest himself from evil by separating his soul from matter and returning
to its original union with the universal Soul. As man could
very well not get rid of his own body, he had to separate himself from it by an ecstatic vision of the Good that required him
closing his eyes to all terrestrial things, including his body, and

---

[299] Plotinus, 2013a, V, 1, 1
[300] Genesis 3:5

by purifying himself through the means of a mystical contemplation:

> The organ of vision will first have to be rendered analogous and similar to the object it is to contemplate. Never would the eye have seen the sun unless first it had assumed its form; likewise, the soul could never see beauty, unless she herself first became beautiful. To obtain the view of the beautiful, and of the divinity, every man must begin by rendering himself beautiful and divine.[301]

There was yet another method for ascending to the Good that, rather than being mystical, was intellectual. It was the philosopher's method. The philosopher first engaged in the study of "... mathematics, so as to accustom him to think of incorporeal things, to believe in their existence..."[302]. In other words, mathematics trained the philosopher's mind to think in a purely theoretical manner with no reference to empirical observations to validate it. Next, the philosopher pursued dialectics as a superior form of reasoning, which Plotinus went on to define as follows:

> What then is this dialectics, knowledge of which must be added to mathematics? It is a science which makes us capable of reasoning about each thing... This science treats also of good and evil; of everything that is subordinated to (being), the Good, and to its contrary; of the nature of what is eternal, and transitory. It treats of each matter scientifically, and not according to mere opinion. Instead of wandering around the sense-world, it establishes itself in the intelligible world; it concentrates its whole attention on this world, and after having saved our soul from deceit, dialectics "pastures our soul in the meadow of truth", (as thought Plato)...[303]

---

[301] Plotinus, 2013a, I, 6, 9
[302] Plotinus, 2013a, I, 3, 3
[303] Plotinus, 2013a, I, 3, 4

To reach such knowledge, dialects relied purely on the deductive method of logic, always remaining on an intangible plane. Since it disregarded terrestrial matters and was purely concerned with the intelligible world, it made no reference to empirical data gained from observations. For Plotinus, the world in which we live did not exist, only the intelligible world existed; thought was identical to existence.[304]

Summary

As may be expected, there were elements in Plotinus that must have had a special appeal to Christian thinkers of his era. Chief among them was his concern with ethics, a theme that carries on from the classical moral philosophy of Plato and Aristotle. In this way, Greek philosophy and Christianity became allies very early and went on to provide the ethical foundation for Western culture. People who blame Christianity and the Bible for the poor behaviour of Christians must realise that fairness demands that the blame should be equally shared by Plato, Aristotle, Plotinus and other philosophers of the same vein.

Another concept paralleling Christian theology is Plotinus' idea that the divinity consisted of a trinity, even if it was an impersonal one. As we have said, the explanation of the three persons in monotheism was something that the Early Fathers, in contrast to the Apostles, felt a need to explain logically to the Hellenic world. Plotinus provided the tools to do this.

Finally, the separation of the soul from the body and the intelligible world from the sense-world would have also been regarded as a logical explanation for Jesus' promise of eternal life in a New Jerusalem.

---

[304] Plotinus, 2013a, V, 9, 5. This was a common assumption of Greek philosophy. As we shall see later, it had an impact not only on theology but on the development of science in general. It placed knowledge obtained through theory above that gained through empirical observation.

10 Origen

Having examined in the prior chapter some relevant traits of neo-platonism, we can now return to the Early Fathers and Origen to assess the extent that he borrowed from neo-platonism to build his theology. Origen has been praised for "his theological brilliance and exegetical insight..."[305]. Among his extensive works in biblical scholarship is the Hexaplorum[306], a monumental work that sets out in columns, side by side, different translations of the Old Testament including the Hebrew version. No doubt the magnitude of his work is proof of a serious commitment to the Scriptures. Yet, despite his voluminous biblical scholarship, he took unbelievable liberties in interpreting Scripture and hammered into it a large dose of neo-platonism with the greatest enthusiasm.

Biblical Interpretation

To carry out the import of neo-platonism into Scripture, Origen proposed three ways of reading the Bible:

> The way... to deal with the Scriptures, and extract from them their meaning, is the following, which has been ascertained from the Scriptures themselves. By Solomon in the Proverbs we find some such rule as this enjoined respecting the divine doctrines of Scripture: "And do thou portray them in a threefold manner, in counsel and knowledge, to answer words of truth to them who propose them to thee." [Proverbs 22:20-21]... For as man consists of body, and soul, and spirit, so in the same way does Scripture, which has been arranged to be given by God for the salvation of men.[307]

Interestingly, Origen's citation is from the Greek OT version and not from the original Hebrew. Moreover, his rendering of

---

[305] Lyman, 2009, p. 417
[306] Field, 1875
[307] Schaff, n.d.d., De Principiis IV, I, 11

"in a threefold manner" for the expression "thrice" (*tris*, G515) in the Greek OT version of Proverbs 22:20 is inaccurate. And the word "thrice" is absent altogether in the original Hebrew OT.

Origen's three modes of biblical interpretation were based on the neo-platonic threefold division of man. This in itself shows how far he was prepared to go to twist the meaning of Scripture to match it with external ideas. The first mode of interpretation, the one for the human body, was based on the literal meaning. There was nothing wrong in reading the literal meaning in most of Scripture, except that Origen regarded such passages as meant for "those who are yet children in soul, and not able to call God their Father..."[308]. In fact, many such passages that can be understood literally are rather profound and go over the heads of infantile minds.

But Origen erred further. His second method of interpretation he said could only be grasped by those whose soul was mature. This method was applied to passages that used metaphors, he explained that:

> there are certain passages of Scripture which do not at all contain the "corporeal" sense, as we shall show in the following (paragraphs), there are also places where we must seek only for the "soul," as it were, and "spirit" of Scripture... [Of such interpretation] there is an illustration in Paul's first Epistle to the Corinthians... "Thou shalt not muzzle the mouth of the ox that treadeth out the corn;" [1 Corinthians 9:9 and Deuteronomy 25:4]...[309]

But, metaphors in the Bible – as in other literature – had exactly the opposite purpose suggested by Origen. Metaphors made an argument self-evident and thus understandable by anyone regardless of the maturity of their soul. In the Corinthians passage, Paul sought to make it plain that if the law stipulated that an ox should be permitted to feed from its labour,

---

[308] Schaff, n.d.d., De Principiis IV, I, 11
[309] Schaff, n.d.d., De Principiis IV, I, 12

the more so should men like himself be allowed to sustain themselves by their work.

While the first two methods were limited to stipulating what type of people were addressed in particular biblical texts, the third method went beyond this. It consisted of finding a "spiritual" meaning in the Bible despite there being no evidence that the authors intended such a meaning. This not only applied to some sections of the Bible, but to its entirety:

> with respect to holy Scripture, our opinion is that the whole of it has a "spiritual," but not the whole a "bodily" meaning, because the bodily meaning is in many places proved to be impossible.[310]

What Origin is saying above is that the whole of the Bible admits a "spiritual" interpretation which can then be used to interpret passages that do not admit – according to him – a literal interpretation. This gave Origen a carte blanche to force into the text of Scripture neo-platonic material that was entirely foreign to the text, such as the case with Proverbs 22:20 mentioned above. In some instances, such as with the Song of Songs, it resulted in an absurd defacing of an entire book.

Due to the extreme attitudes on both sides that society has applied to sexuality – abstention and overindulgence – the Song of Songs has always been an important book of the Bible. All people, especially the young should read it and have it explained to them. Regretfully, Origen adopted the extreme attitudes to sexuality that did not accept sensual love between a man and a woman as being the work of God. For him, anyone who received the meaning of this book literally was "carnal":

> For he, not knowing how to hear love's language in purity and with chaste ears, will twist the whole manner of his hearing of it away from the inner spiritual man and on to the outward and carnal... and it will seem to be the Divine Scriptures that are thus urging and egging him on to fleshly lust![311]

---

[310] Schaff, n.d.d., De Principiis IV, I, 20
[311] Origen, 1957, p. 22

Origen was not the first to interpret this book in a manner that avoided its sexual and sensual theme. It had been done by rabbis prior to the Christian era. However, he established a precedent in Christian biblical interpretation by applying his spiritual method. He assumed that mention of parts of the human body in this book ought to be understood as referring "to the parts and powers of the invisible soul."[312] Thus the bride's cheeks in Song of Songs 1:10 are "those members of the Church who cultivate the integrity of chastity and virtue."[313] And her neck in the same verse "must surely denote those souls who receive the yoke of Christ..."[314]

But Origen's method of spiritual interpretation went far beyond passages that contained sensual language. He established the criterion that a passage of the Bible ought to be interpreted spiritually:

> when one is able to show of what heavenly things... and of what future blessings the [OT] law contains a shadow.[315]

What he regarded as "heavenly things" and "future blessings" was strongly influenced by neo-platonism as we shall see in the next section.

Two Worlds

Origen's conception of the world ran parallel to neo-platonism, but with some variations to incorporate biblical ideas. His method of biblical interpretation served him well for this purpose. Like Plotinus, Origen believed in two worlds, one invisible and the other visible, that is, the one which we recognise as the Creation. These two worlds were created by a God who was "an uncompounded intellectual nature..."[316], a pure mind

---

[312] Origen, 1957, p. 28
[313] Origen, 1957, p. 145f
[314] Origen, 1957, p.146
[315] Schaff, n.d.d., De Principiis IV, I, 13
[316] Schaff, n.d.d., De Principiis I, I, 6

much like "the One" of Plotinus. The creation of the invisible world, said Origen, preceded the creation of the visible:

> not... for the first time did God begin to work when He made this visible world; but as, after its destruction, there will be another world, so also we believe that *others existed before the present came into being.*[317]

He suggested other invisible worlds, but we shall only deal with the one whence humanity proceeded. For he believed that man existed in the form of a "rational creature" prior to the creation of the visible world:

> In that commencement... God created so great a number of *rational or intellectual creatures* (or by whatever name they are to be called), which we have *formerly termed understandings*, as He foresaw would be sufficient.[318]

Thus, Origen followed the Platonic and neo-platonic tradition by placing the intellect of man outside the Creation. By slipping this idea into his theology, he set a precedent for the future development of Western thought. It shaped not only theology but philosophy and the sciences as well. Though he would not have agreed with it, modernism did something very similar when it deified science, making it become something autonomous and transcending ordinary human qualities. People were expected to revere it and bend to its prescripts when in truth there never has been such things as autonomous science. What there has always been is human thinking as an integral part of man's flesh and blood and squarely placed within the Creation.

Next, Origen went on to tell us – similarly to Plotinus – how some of these rational creatures became flesh and blood men. He explains that in Scripture God was called "a fire", but some rational creatures strayed from their love of this "fire" and became "cold":

---

[317] Schaff, n.d.d., De Principiis III, V, 3; emphasis added
[318] Schaff, n.d.d., De Principiis II, IX, 1; emphasis added

> As God, then, is a fire, and the angels a flame of fire,
> and all the saints are fervent in spirit, so, on the con-
> trary, *those who have fallen away from the love of God
> are undoubtedly said to have cooled* in their affection
> for Him, and to have become cold. For the Lord also
> says, that, "because iniquity has abounded, the love of
> many will grow cold." [Matthew 24:12][319]

Since the Scriptures speak of the soul by censuring it rather
than praising it, he deduced that the rational creature "falling
away from its status and dignity, was made or named
soul..."[320]. The fall of man, therefore, began in his soul prior to
the creation of the visible world, in fact, Origen believed that
the visible world was created as a consequence of this fall:

> *to those souls which, on account of their excessive
> mental defects*, stood in need of bodies of a grosser and
> more solid nature; and for the sake of those for whom
> this arrangement was necessary, *this visible world was
> also called into being.*[321]

And he regarded the visible world as inferior to the invisible
world:

> there has been a *descent from a higher to a lower con-
> dition*, on the part not only of those souls who have de-
> served the change by the variety of their movements,
> but also on that of those who, in order to serve the
> whole world, were *brought down from those higher
> and invisible spheres to these lower and visible
> ones...*[322]

He sought evidence for this inferiority by claiming that the
Greek word *katabole* (G2602) used in the expression *foundation of the* world in the NT[323] was incorrectly rendered. According to him, the correct meaning of *katabole* was "to cast

---

[319] Schaff, n.d.d., De Principiis II, VIII, 3; emphasis added
[320] Schaff, n.d.d., De Principiis II, VIII, 3
[321] Schaff, n.d.d., De Principiis III, V, 4; emphasis added
[322] Schaff, n.d.d., De Principiis III, V, 4; emphasis added.
[323] E.g. Matthew 13:35; Ephesians 1:4

downwards". Therefore, these verses should be translated as *the casting down of the world* rather than *the foundation of the world*. Such low esteem for the Creation was accompanied by a similar attitude to the human body. He not only considered it was made "of a grosser and more solid nature"[324], but since the Bible stated that "the Creation was subjected to vanity..."[325], Origen concluded that vanity was "nothing else than the body..."[326].

The Logos

Like other Early Fathers with a philosophical and theological bent, Origen speculated mostly with an abstract notion of Jesus which he thought lay behind the term Logos. In this he went against the trend of his society, for:

> Popular feeling in the East.... [that] wanted to have a God on earth who walks with us, not a divine transcendent power who merely takes on flesh, and then returns after he has taken it on.[327]

This feeling in the passage quoted above, was not limited to the East nor to the times of Origen. It is a perennial human need that the Bible addresses with the advent of Christ. We must stress this. The people needed a flesh and blood redeemer, someone who not only was born, lived, died on earth, but also resurrected from it. To confirm the latter, he was seen repeatedly for forty days after his death[328] and by more than five hundred people[329].

Periods of time that cover forty days or years occur several times in the Bible[330]. Many such occurrences point to inordin-

---

[324] Schaff, n.d.d., De Principiis III, V, 4
[325] Romans 8:20-21
[326] Schaff, n.d.d., De Principiis I, VII, 5
[327] Tillich, 1968, p. 62
[328] Acts 1:3
[329] 1 Corinthians 15:6
[330] It rained for forty days and nights during Noah's time, Genesis 7:4, Israel wandered for forty years in the desert, Numbers 14:33 and Jesus spent forty days without food in the wilderness, Matthew 4:2.

ately long periods of time. We can gather that Jesus was seen for forty days, rather than for a week or fortnight, to prove beyond reasonable doubt that his body was the same that hung on the cross. When he appeared before his disciples he insisted he was not spirit or ghost. He was real. He showed them his hands and feet, told them to touch him and even asked for food and ate it[331]. He challenged Thomas to touch the scars of his wounds[332]. It all demonstrated that the incarnation was an historical event within the Creation both before and after Jesus' death and resurrection and even at the time of his ascension[333]. Everything that is humanly needed to know about Christ took place within the scope of history and within the Creation.

Origen, however, had other ideas. He strongly rejected Paul's affirmation[334] that in Jesus dwelt the fullness of God:

> it is monstrous and unlawful to compare God the Father, in the generation of His only-begotten Son, and in the substance of the same, to any man or other living thing engaged in such an act...[335]

He believed that Jesus had two natures, one was his soul and the other his body. His soul was "like an iron in the fire... perpetually placed in the Word [Logos], and perpetually in the Wisdom, and perpetually in God..."[336]. However, only his soul was incarnate, but not the Word:

> This substance of a soul, then, being intermediate between God and the flesh – it being impossible for the nature of God to intermingle with a body without an intermediate instrument – God-man is born...[337]

---

[331] Luke 24:38-43
[332] John 20:27
[333] Acts 1:9,11
[334] Colossians 1:19, 2:9; Philippians 2:5-8
[335] Schaff, n.d.d., De Principiis I, II, 4
[336] Schaff, n.d.d., De Principiis II, VI, 6. Origen often wrote "Reason" as synonym of "Word", which gave Christ's soul a rationalistic tint resembling Plotinus universal Intelligence.
[337] Schaff, n.d.d., De Principiis II, VI, 3

Moreover, Origen believed that Jesus assumed human nature only temporarily "for the purposes of the dispensation (of grace)..."[338]. And he did not believe that Jesus had been bodily taken up at the ascension. He warned people:

> Let ours be the more reverent conception of the ascension of the Son to the Father with sanctified insight, an ascension rather of soul than of body.[339]

Origen thus embraced the Early Fathers' persistent endeavour to devalue the body, in the typical Hellenic tradition, despite the biblical witness to the contrary[340]. Combined with his low esteem for the Creation, he unwittingly brought humanity down by robbing men and women of their purpose in life, both here and thereafter – a life that Jesus had claimed he had come to restore in abundance[341]. And finally, rather than seeing God's Spirit as enveloping the Creation and intervening in everything that happens in it, Origen drastically limited his sphere of activity:

> I am of opinion... that the operation of the Holy Spirit does not take place at all in those things which are without life, or in those which, although living, are yet dumb; nay, is not found even in those who are endued indeed with reason, but are engaged in evil courses, and not at all converted to a better life. In those persons alone do I think that the operation of the Holy Spirit takes place, who are already turning to a *better life*, and walking along the way which leads to Jesus Christ, i.e., who are engaged in the performance of *good actions*, and who abide in God.[342]

---

[338] Schaff, n.d.d., De Principiis I, II, 1
[339] Origen, n.d., XIII
[340] Paul regards the body as belonging to Christ and as the temple of the Holy Spirit, 1 Corinthians 3:6; 6:15, 9. Since the Holy Spirit is the worker that sustains the Creation, we must understand his dwelling in our body to drive us to work and to use our brains, since the latter is also part of the temple.
[341] John 10:10
[342] Schaff, n.d.d., De Principiis I, III, 5; emphasis added

Theology and Science

It does not seem that Origen had in mind that "a better life" and "good actions" should translate into anything practical. For he looked down upon Creation and encouraged people to step out of it and instead dedicate themselves to a mystical communion with God. Like Plotinus, Origen's idea of communion was purely an intellectual exercise:

> we ought to despise things "sensible," and "temporal," and "visible," and to do our utmost to reach communion with God, and the contemplation of things that are "intelligent," and "invisible," and a blessed life with God, and the friends of God...[343]

Even his reading of Scripture was bound in mysticism, encouraging people to have their "minds chastened and educated by the *mystical contemplation* of the law and the prophets." [344] He did not put as much stress on practising what both the law and the prophets prescribed.

Along with this and motivated by his belief that the body was inferior to the soul, Origen espoused a strict ascetic attitude. In particular he rejected sexual desire and held to other restrictions of a Hellenic origin like his predecessors. He condemned, as we have seen, succumbing to "carnality" and literally reading the Song of Solomon to learn about the bodily pleasures that God had given to man and wife. This mysticism and disdain for the body and the Creation was also extended to intellectual matters. Here he defined three types of wisdom: (1) the wisdom of the world, (2) the wisdom of the princes of the world and (3) the wisdom of God[345]. He supported this division by referring to the following passage written by Paul:

> Howbeit we speak wisdom among the perfect: yet a wisdom not of this world, nor of the rulers of this world, which are coming to nought...[346]

[343] Schaff, n.d.d., Against Celsus III, LVI
[344] Schaff, n.d.d., Against Celsus II, VI; emphasis added
[345] Schaff, n.d.d., De Principiis III, III, 1
[346] 1 Corinthians 2:6

But he misinterpreted this passage – like many others. Paul was highlighting the wisdom of God. The mention of the other types of wisdom is purely for the purpose of contrast. For Paul, there was only God's wisdom and folly[347]. The folly of princes, such as Pharaoh or Herod, was the same as the folly of their subjects.

Yet, this is a minor point. Of far greater bearing is Origen's view that wisdom could be found at different levels. Paul polarised human thought into God's wisdom and folly and saw God's wisdom and man's folly as opposed to each other with nothing in between. Origen, on the other hand, perceived shades of grey in between. He placed God's wisdom at the highest level and defined it as the seeking of "divine things"[348] and the study of philosophy. We gather that for him philosophy covered "the plan of the world's government, or any other subjects of importance, or regarding the training for a good or happy life..."[349]. These, together with divinity, were for Origen the subject matter of godly wisdom.

However, in order that people who did not partake of God's wisdom should not "altogether neglect the cultivation of their minds..."[350], God created in them a great number of needs. These needs led them in turn to invent the arts and sciences to satisfy them. They comprised the wisdom of the world, something in between God's wisdom and human folly. Origen wrote that this worldly wisdom:

> deals wholly with the art of poetry, e.g., or that of grammar, or rhetoric, or geometry, or music, with which also, perhaps, medicine should be classed. In all these subjects we are to suppose that the wisdom of this world is included.[351]

---

[347] 1 Corinthians 3:19
[348] Schaff, n.d.d., Against Celsus IV, LXXVI
[349] Schaff, n.d.d., De Principiis III, III, 2
[350] Schaff, n.d.d., Against Celsus IV, LXXVI
[351] Schaff, n.d.d., De Principiis III, III, 2

The above mentioned sciences were a product of man, they were not a gift of God as the Bible affirms[352]. Origen thus established a dividing wall between theology on the one hand, and the natural and human sciences on the other. The former dealt with the wisdom of God and the invisible world, the latter with the visible world and its worldly wisdom. He was not the sole builder of this wall; his predecessors had started to erect it before him. But he certainly buttressed it by providing an alternative methodology for theology that released it from the need to provide empirical evidence to support its speculations. This methodology has protected theologians to this day by establishing a comfortable divide: they see the Christian dimension as a religion and think that science belongs to the secular world. An illustration of the defence of this divide is found in an interview with Paul Tillich conducted at Union Theological Seminary (USA) in 1956:

> if you define faith as belief in something more or less believable, then you are continuously in conflict with history, with natural science, with psychology, with everything. At the moment in which you say that faith is being ultimately concerned and that the religious expressions are symbols, then there is no interference of science with religion and of religion with science. They are in two different dimensions; science is the dimension of describing this reality in all its relations to each other. Religion points to the dimension of the ultimate and in this way there is no possible conflict if this is seen in a clear way.[353]

Although Tillich represents one pole of the theological spectrum, similar views can be found in almost every denomination of Christianity.

---

[352] Exodus 31:2-5; 1 Kings 4:29-33
[353] National Council of Churches of Christ, USA, 1956

Conclusion

Despite the fact that Origen was Clement's student and that they shared a common intellectual background in Alexandria, their ideas were markedly dissimilar. In fact, if we refer once more to Table 3-1, we will see that Origen reversed almost every intellectual contribution that Clement had made towards promoting biblical Christendom. By splitting the world in two, Origen shifted the Christian vision from the Creation to the invisible world and from Christendom to religion. His lower regard for science – as mere wisdom of the world – meant that what people believed, including himself, could never be brought under the critical examination of the sciences. Orthodoxy, or the rule of truth, could not be challenged – just as Tillich expected in modern times. This also split the educational agenda commissioned by Christ[354]. On the one hand, it was inevitable that the sciences would be handed over to worldly institutions with syllabi devoid of "subjects of importance, or regarding the training for a good or happy life". One wonders how Origen expected that, despite this kind of exclusion, students would nevertheless have their minds cultivated. One must presume that, since such subjects belonged to the wisdom of God, they were to be delivered by the clergy through indoctrination. People were to be preached at, not taught in the proper pedagogical sense of the word.

Finally, Origen's low esteem for the Creation and man's body meant that goodness was to be sought in the invisible world and by disengaging oneself from the body and from the Creation. Goodness was not to be sought through work but through mystical contemplation. Goodness and work were to be exchanged for asceticism and worship.

---

[354] Matthew 28:19-20

11 Cyprian

Introduction

From Alexandria, the seat of Christian philosophy and theology, we travel once more to the organisationally-oriented Carthage to meet Cyprian, its bishop and the last of the Early Church Fathers we will examine. At this stage we are in the middle of the 3rd century, an era marked by controversy within the church began by the persecution of Christians under the emperor Decius in 250. The controversy was about how to deal with the Christians who had given into the brutal stamping out of Christianity by Rome and had forcibly renounced their faith. Once the persecution subsided, some of the priests in Carthage issued pardons without the authority of the bishop. Cyprian saw this as a challenge, not only to him but to the episcopal system in general, and led him to produce letters and treatises defending the authority of the bishop and the unity of the church. Another issue that began to raise its head at this time was the ascendency of the bishop of Rome over the other bishops. While Cyprian regarded Rome as the ancient seat of Peter, it is unclear from his writings whether he supported the primacy of the bishop of Rome or not. Opinion about this varies. Roman Catholic scholars, as expected, claim that Cyprian saw himself as being subordinate to the bishop of Rome. Protestant scholars on the other hand, thought Cyprian was defending the autonomy of each bishop to govern his own diocese. The documents that are available support the second position.

In addition to church authority, Cyprian was the first major figure of the church to ascribe a sacerdotal[355] role to the clergy, that is, he regarded them as priests who offered a sacrifice at the celebration of the Lord's supper. This represents a major shift in the church's focus, for "until Cyprian's time the church constantly boasted in its dealing with pagans that it had neither altar nor sacrifice."[356] After this, altars and sacrifices took a

---

[355] By sacerdotal I mean a priest who offers a sacrifice on behalf of himself and others.
[356] Renwick, 1968, p. 43

centre stage position in the church's activities and further displaced the business of addressing the concrete problems of humanity.

Episcopal Organisation

There was little that Cyprian added about the authority of the bishop over the church that was not already expressed by Ignatius more than a century earlier. He reasserted the right of a bishop to deal autonomously with the matters of his own regional church and to exercise his authority over it. Ignatius, however, did not have to deal with a bishop of Rome who considered himself above the others. Stephen, who served as bishop of Rome between 254 and 257, introduced a new level in the hierarchy when he claimed to have authority over the other bishops. The claim was based on (1) Jesus' words to Peter in Matthew 16:18[357], (2) the belief, held by Cyprian himself that the apostles were bishops[358] and (3) that Peter was the first bishop of Rome. We must keep in mind, however, that in the NT the task of an apostle was different to the one of the bishop. An apostle was a transient office[359], while a bishop – also called elder – served as an overseer[360] and was therefore a localised appointment. It is most unlikely that Peter, being an apostle, served as bishop of Rome.

Moreover, while it is likely that initially Jesus had Peter in mind to spearhead the evangelical mission of the church, he did not prove equal to the task. He tended to lose his nerve under opposition[361]. It is not unusual in biblical history that God's chosen leaders failed to meet his expectations. In such cases, God replaced them with bolder leaders; Moses was replaced by Joshua, Saul by David and Peter gave way to Paul, who had

---

[357] "thou art Peter, and upon this rock I will build my church..."
[358] Schaff, n.d.e., Epistle LXIV, 3
[359] The Greek word in the original is *apostolos* (G652) meaning "messenger, ambassador, envoy", LSJ.
[360] Overseer is the literal meaning of the Greek word *episkopos* (G1985) in the original documents, LSJ.
[361] Matthew 26:75; Galatians 2:11-12

courage and nerve to spare. And history tells us that Paul, rather than Peter, first reached Rome and started his evangelical mission while being imprisoned at home.   Finally, if a particular community deserved to have a special place as the foundation of the church, it should have been Antioch rather than Rome. As we have seen, not only did Antioch send and support Paul and Barnabas on their first mission[362], it was the place where the church was first consolidated into a substantial community after it had been dispersed from Jerusalem[363].

Thus, the Roman claim for supremacy was not rooted in having been historically a foundation-church; this claim was most probably something engineered later. It satisfied a bureaucratic appetite – that one can imagine was preponderant in Rome – to centralise power and control in a place of prominence. Undoubtedly, the city of Rome was far more prestigious than Antioch. One wonders whether the bishops heading churches in places other than Rome saw through all this and thus refused to relinquish their autonomy. Bishop Stephen's move was met with firm resistance from his colleagues, who responded in a rather irate manner. Cyprian wrote:

> For *neither does any of us set himself up as a bishop of bishops, nor by tyrannical terror does any compel his colleague to the necessity of obedience*; since every bishop, according to the allowance of his liberty and power, has his own proper right of judgement, and can no more be judged by another than he himself can judge another.[364]

Likewise, Firmilian, bishop of Caesarea did not mince words in rebuking Stephen for his daring claim:

> And in this respect *I am justly indignant at this so open and manifest folly of Stephen*, that he... boasts of the place of his episcopate, and contends that he holds the

---

[362] Acts 13:1-3
[363] Acts 11:20-26
[364] Schaff, n.d.e., The Seventh Council of Carthage under Cyprian; emphasis added

succession from Peter, [Matt. xvi. 19] on whom the foundations of the Church were laid...[365]

In fact, Cyprian interpreted Matthew 16:18 in the opposite way, as supporting a distributed episcopal system, which as a whole formed the foundation of the church:

> There is easy proof [in Matt. 16:18-19] for... [a]... unity we ought firmly to hold and assert, especially those of us that are bishops who preside in the Church, that we may also prove the episcopate itself to be one and undivided.[366]

All of this demonstrates the gradual and ever advancing move away from the NT church as a community, structured in a familial manner, towards a centralised bureaucracy. Even if at some point in time regional bishops were still defending their autonomy from Rome, they themselves had already begun the process of bureaucratic centralisation within their own regional churches which would eventually justify Rome's claim.

The rigid bureaucratic aspirations of the bishops was often concealed under such pious terms as "Mother Church". Given that Cyprian was the "spiritual son and pupil of Tertullian"[367] one can deduce that by the Mother Church he meant the clergy standing above the people. Despite the familial sound of the word "Mother", what Cyprian had in mind was a bureaucratic organisation, which he reaffirmed by his extolling virginity and thereby undermining marriage and family:

> My address is now to *virgins, whose glory, as it is more eminent, excites the greater interest. This is the flower of the ecclesiastical seed*, the grace and ornament of spiritual endowment, a joyous disposition, the wholesome and uncorrupted work of praise and honour, God's image answering to the holiness of the Lord, the more illustrious portion of Christ's flock. The glorious

---

[365] Schaff, n.d.e., Epistle LXXIV, 17; emphasis added
[366] Schaff, n.d.e., Treatise I, 4 & 5
[367] Schaff, n.d.e., Introductory Notice to Cyprian

> fruitfulness of Mother Church rejoices by their means,
> and in them abundantly flourishes; and in proportion as
> a copious virginity is added to her number, so much the
> more it increases the joy of the Mother.[368]

Virginity and celibacy – understood as the opposites of marriage – carried with them individualism, a necessary ingredient of a bureaucracy. It provided the flexibility needed to organise people as it most suited the bureaucratic purpose, without the encumbrances of wives, husbands and children. I do not think that Cyprian consciously sought to extol virginity to pursue bureaucratic objectives, but I assume that he was merely adopting the Greco-Roman form of organisation with which he was most acquainted. And the greatest problem that eventually arose from this organisation is that the church's mission was placed on the shoulders of the clergy who became "the ministers of the Church"[369], that is the servants. The laity became the served, releasing them from any responsibility to carry out Christ's work beyond living a moral personal life and obeying the clergy. It created a dependant attitude among Christians – reinforced by the word "Mother" – where the church played the role of a spiritual nanny.

Religion Abolished

Although Cyprian was not the first to refer to the Christian faith as a "religion" – Tertullian and Origen also spoke of it as such[370] – he made some momentous additions to it based on misunderstanding the OT. Both the OT and NT had God's people as the focus of the events they narrate. What united the people and gave them their identity throughout this narration was God's law, not religion. In fact, not all religious ceremonies that were incorporated in the OT had their origins in the Hebrew culture alone. Egyptians and Canaanites also had

---

[368] Schaff, n.d.e., Treatise II, 3; emphasis added
[369] Schaff, n.d.e., Epistle XXVII, 3
[370] See for example Tertullian, Schaff, n.d.c., The Five Books Against Marcion, IV, IV and Origen Schaff, n.d.d., De Principiis IV, I, 2

priests, altars and temples dedicated to their deities. The OT incorporated some of these practices but radically changed their meaning. Israel's religious ceremonies were not aimed at promoting fertility or winning over the favour of God. He was always on Israel's side[371]. The most important objective of these ceremonies was atonement for the people's transgression of the law. This was marked by placing the law tablets in the Holies of Holies, the most honoured position in the temple. While the OT stipulated other religious rituals, such as the offerings of thanksgiving and worship, the atonement of sins remained the foremost objective of the religious ceremonies.

As Israel's history unfolded and progressively failed to meet God's expectations – its people having become dissolute and exploitative of the poor – God rejected religious rituals as hypocrisy. He exhorted people to replace ritual with compassion and social justice[372] and announced a new covenant to attain them. In the new covenant the law would not be written in tablets and placed in a temple but would be written in the hearts of the people who, in turn, would become the temple[373]. This is the covenant that Christ introduced and which made all religious practices obsolete. His death was the last sacrifice required, for it atoned for the sins of people once and for all. No more sacrifices were needed after it:

> by one offering he [Christ] hath perfected for ever them that are sanctified. And the Holy Ghost also beareth witness to us: for after he hath said, This is the covenant that I will make with them After those days, saith the Lord; I will put my laws on their heart, And upon their mind also will I write them; then saith he, And their sins and their iniquities will I remember no more. Now where remission of these is, there is no more offering for sin.[374]

---

[371] Deuteronomy 4:7
[372] Isaiah 1:11-17
[373] Jeremiah 31:33-34
[374] Hebrews 10:14-18

Therefore, the new covenant between God and his people made religion, priests, altars and temples obsolete. That is why the NT never speaks of the Christian faith as a religion[375]. A great portion of James' epistle[376] is dedicated to explaining the substitution of the old religion by a "pure religion" that meant work and a pure mind. People were now expected to show their faith by their work starting with relieving the burden of the most vulnerable in society. In the spirit of Isaiah, James instructed his people not to insult the poor, not to exploit them and not to deny them justice. He exhorted them to take corrective action and to get to work. Although God did not forgive his people's transgressions because of their work, nevertheless, having freely forgiven them he demanded work from them. Working for humanity replaced altars, sacrifices and priests. The new "priesthood"[377] offered their sacrifice through their work for the betterment of humanity. It is in this context we should understand Paul's exhortation to the Romans:

> For of him, and through him, and unto him, are all things. To him be the glory for ever. Amen
> I beseech you therefore, brethren, by the mercies of God, to present *your bodies a living sacrifice*, holy, acceptable to God, which is your *reasonable service*[378].

One should note two points in this passage. The first is that it began with an affirmation of Christ's total sovereignty over his Creation. It echoed Paul's words to the Colossians affirming not only the redemption of man, but of all the Creation, with man included in it and not apart from it. It was a comprehensive redemption that in today's vernacular, people would call a "package deal". It was not a redemption of separate parts, but of a whole. It should be also understood that the objective of the redemption was the restoration of all things to their original state, that is, just as they were created in the beginning. And while the redemption was fully accomplished at the time

---

[375] In the NT Christ's deeds and teachings are never referred to as pertaining to religion, but to the kingdom of God, Matthew 4:23.
[376] James 1:22-2:26
[377] 1 Peter 2:5,9
[378] Romans 11:36-12:1

of Christ's death, the restoration work was – and is – still in progress. One could envisage redemption as being the demolition of an old dilapidated building which has been completed and the restoration as the erection of the new building which is still in the construction stage. Thus, just as man in the beginning was put to work in the garden of Eden, so now he was put to work in the restoration process of the Creation. And his first task was to move the poor and indigent out of their misery into a dignified form of life.

This brings us to the second point. Paul said that the work of restoration demanded a sacrifice that was reasonable[379], that is, that made sense. For changing the world required far more effort than the compensation received in exchange. Thus rather than offering sacrifices before an altar, the new priesthood of all believers was meant to roll up its sleeves and get its hands dirty with the materials needed to build a new community. That was the work that God had ordained them to do[380]. This ought to have excited people, especially the young. The wide scope of the people's needs, as Jesus saw it[381], was a challenge to the workers. It required vast learning, skill and creativity to address such needs and this meant an opportunity to live human life to the full, here on earth, within God's own Creation, just as he had mandated it in the beginning[382].

Religion Reintroduced

This is a vision that most of the Early Fathers and the clergy, with the exception of people such as Clement of Alexandria, did definitely, not understand. They failed to capture the vastness of Christ's mission and persisted in pressing it down into a religious mould – controlled by bishop and clergy – that smothered people's initiative rather than encouraged it.

---

[379] I think a more accurate translation would be *intelligent service*. The Greek word in the original is *logikos* (G3050) which literally means rational or logical, MIC.

[380] Ephesians 2:10

[381] Matthew 9:36-37

[382] Genesis 1:28-31; 2:15

Rather than making life abundant, they made it meagre. I think this was motivated in part by the inability of their minds to grasp a redemption that embraced the totality of the Creation; their thoughts were too much soaked in Greek philosophy and tradition. The very notion of the Creation was foreign to the Greek. It was difficult for them to comprehend that a physical world, comprised of earth, water, trees, animals and every other creature, could please God. And therefore they, like Plotinus, sought an invisible world which they mistakenly associated with the biblical kingdom of heaven.

Cyprian added to this process by rolling back history and endeavouring to shape the clergy after the OT Levites. Since the Levites were not apportioned land like the other tribes, they had to be supported by the other tribes; this allowed the Levites to devote themselves exclusively to priestly functions[383]. Cyprian thought the same arrangement should be instituted in the church:

> All which was done by divine authority and arrangement, so that they who waited on divine services might in no respect be called away, nor be compelled to consider or to transact *secular business*. Which plan and rule is now maintained *in respect of the clergy*, that they who are promoted by clerical ordination in the Church of the Lord may be called off in no respect from the divine administration, nor be *tied down by worldly anxieties and matters*; but in the honour of the brethren who contribute, receiving as it were *tenths of the fruits*, they may not withdraw from *the altars and sacrifices, but may serve day and night in heavenly and spiritual things*.[384]

Thus, Cyprian expected the clergy to be sustained by people who were involved in "secular business" and who were "tied down by worldly anxieties and matters". This either meant that clergy ate bread earned through the illicit activities of the laity – illicit at least in the eyes of God – or it meant that such activ-

---

[383] Numbers 18:1-24
[384] Schaff, n.d.e., Epistle LXV, 1

ities were permitted as long as they were performed by the laity. In other words, when it came to matters of economics and work, the laity were encouraged by Cyprian to conform to the pattern of the world[385] in order to provide for the "spiritual" activities of the church[386].

Cyprian also misled the laity by suggesting that only the clergy served "in heavenly and spiritual things". Like Origen, he constrained the sovereignty of God's Spirit to a religious scope. Contrary to the biblical teaching, he would not, for example, have considered work in agriculture or carpentry as "heavenly" or "spiritual". The original biblical word translated as *heaven* in English literally means the sky[387]. When used in the practical context of human activity, it does not point to an invisible world as conceived by Origen, but is used as a metaphor suggesting excellence or loftiness. Accordingly, one can regard as spiritual any good work that is put together with love and dedication and that serves humanity. It does not make any difference whether it is a wooden chair or a symphony.

Finally, there is the reference to "altars and sacrifices". As we have seen, speculations about the Lord's Supper began with Justin, but Cyprian took matters a step further. He replaced the supper with a sacrifice and the table with an altar and claimed that Jesus had taught this[388]. Over the centuries, this generated an ongoing debate among theologians, especially as further speculations were added regarding the "real presence" of Christ in the bread and the wine. These are matters that do not concern us here, of greater importance and impact to humanity was the religious character that Cyprian attributed to sacrifice and the impact it had on the life of Christians. He either ritualised sacrifice by excluding the sweat of work or he narrowed it

---

[385] This is contrary to Paul's advice in Romans 12:2.

[386] Romans 12:2: this applies not only to Cyprian's time. It has justified today's Christian layman to consider that "business is business" and uncritically endorse exploitative socio-economic systems such as capitalism and state socialism.

[387] Hebrew *shamayim* (H8064), e.g. Isaiah 66:1 and Greek *ouranos* (G3772), e.g. Matthew 3:2, MIC.

[388] Schaff, n.d.e., Epistle LXII, 1

down to martyrdom as a result of religious persecution[389]. But he did not regard the work that Christians should have performed to improve the lot of humanity – such as in medicine, architecture, education and the various crafts – as a sacrifice fitting the description in Romans 12:1. On the contrary, like Tertullian, he sanctioned a comfortable in-between zone for the laity, where in the absence of religious persecution, they had the best of two worlds. On the one hand, through the "ministry" of the clergy, the laity could think of themselves as in good standing with God and even blessed by him. On the other hand, provided that they adhered to a personal morality and shared a tithe of their earnings, they could conform to the pattern of the world and conduct business as usual.

This comfortable in-between zone has been the major bane of Christendom and of far greater impact than heresy. For Christians who have fallen into this trap – being the greater majority – have sinned in a threefold manner against God and humanity. Firstly, they provide a poor role model for others to imitate, especially the young. Secondly, they have neglected to fight against a socio-economic and juridical system that oppresses the poor. And thirdly, they have added insult to injury to the poor; they have ignored their plight while enjoying the comfort of riches gained by conforming to the pattern of the world.

Summary

Cyprian closed the post-apostolic period we have been following by consolidating the work of his predecessors who turned work into worship and community into bureaucracy (see Table 3-1). Firstly, by introducing sacrifice into the Lord's supper and turning the clergy into a sacerdotal priesthood, he moved further away from the idea of Christendom as a working community. Secondly, he strengthened the autocratic role

---

[389] See Schaff, n.d.e., Epistle LXXVI, 3 and On the Exhortation to Martyrdom, 8, where he cites Romans 12:1 out of context to support his argument.

of the bishop. Although he resisted bishop Stephen's move to place the seat of Rome above the other bishoprics, he indirectly set a precedent for the autocracy that Rome demanded once an extra hierarchical level was introduced into the clergy in later years.

Cyprian died in 258 and by this time the pattern of a Christian religion was firmly established and the biblical vision of Christendom here on earth definitely abandoned. The Early Fathers were never able to rid themselves of their Greek way of thinking and exchange it for the Hebrew historical reasoning with which the Bible was written. The notable exception was Clement of Alexandria, who was insightful enough to use Greek thought to help the mission of the church without compromising its biblical character. Sadly he was all too soon overshadowed by Origen and his work buried under the neo-platonic speculations of his own pupil. The intellectual and cultural impact of all this on Christendom was massive and long lasting. It rendered the church utterly ineffective in stemming off a dark age that the barbarians inaugurated after the fall of Rome. However, that is in the past and nothing can be done about it, except to learn from it. Our concern now is with the darkness of our own age. The task of the next chapter will be to incorporate what we have learned from the past into a model that may enlighten us in the midst of our contemporary darkness.

12 Contemporary Bureaucracy

The Mainstream Church Model

Having completed tracing the transformation of the selected socio-cultural factors in the post-apostolic period, our next task is to transfer them into today's church and see their impact on its competence to face the challenges of neo-liberalism, which I have said above, is the latest expression of modernity. To attain this, we will build a dynamic model with these factors – similar to the ones shown in Figure 3-2 – to represent the contemporary mainstream churches – Roman Catholic, Eastern Orthodox or Protestant denominations– that share the same theological and organisational foundations that developed during the post-apostolic period. The model aims to explain how the church has become a stagnant institution and has been unable to arrest the socio-cultural decline in contemporary society.

To facilitate comparison, I have set this new model side by side with the early church's community model – introduced in Chapter 3 – and labelled it *bureaucratic model* in Figure 12-1. Although the church did not invent bureaucracy, we nevertheless have seen how it adopted it right at the beginning of the post-apostolic period and, with few exceptions, preserved it and provided it as a model for other social institutions to imitate. This model has been assembled with the factors listed at the bottom of Table 3-1 which emerged under the influence of the Early Fathers. We should first note that history is not included in this model, for vision now has become orthodoxy, and orthodoxy is static[390]. Bureaucracy has replaced community as the form of social organisation. I have highlighted it with grey to emphasise that it is the centre of social control. This is in contrast to the community model, where initiatives – rather than control – flow out of vision, and are equipped with competence through education and implemented by work.

---

[390] This is in contrast to the Bible which, being an historical collection of documents, shows the full dynamism of history.

Bureaucratic control is exercised by ensuring that ortho-doxy – the "rule of faith" – remains circumvented to a fixed religious and theological perimeter (arrow 1 in the figure) in contrast to the OT law which spans every aspect of the Cre-ation and of human life. Thus, bureaucracy does not educate, but indoctrinates or catechises (arrow 2) within the perimeter marked by the walls of its orthodoxy (arrow 3).

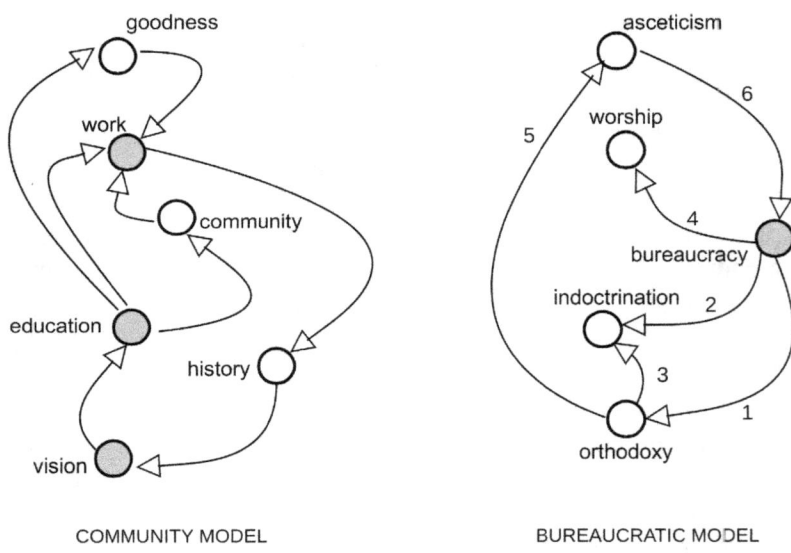

COMMUNITY MODEL   BUREAUCRATIC MODEL

Figure 12-1 Community and Bureaucratic Models

Indoctrination disconnects Christian thought from the rest of the sciences so that it cannot respond to the challenges that humanity faces at each particular point in history. This is based on the Greek idea of a static truth which, as we have seen, was imported into Christianity by the Early Fathers. Biblical truth on the other hand, is focused on historical events driven by what Ortega y Gasset called an invariable historic nucleus[391]. The biblical historic nucleus is shaped by the fall and redemp-tion of man and Creation. This nucleus – which stands for the

---

[391] 1924

philosophy of Christ – provides a grammar to science that dynamically links and articulates the sciences in a similar manner to the way the grammar of a language links and articulates words. This articulation mobilises the sciences to respond to the historical challenges, by serving humanity, by educating it and by organising people into a community of familial structure. On the other hand, indoctrination dismisses science and immobilises thought. The catechetical form of instruction is to ask questions for which answers are ready made. This generates an assembly line intellect that fits well with the organisational structure of a bureaucracy. No doubt, there are questions for which answers are already available, but true education does not stop there. It proceeds to ask further questions for which no answers are yet available and which requires drawing from the sciences, especially the humanities. This teaches students how to think.

Next, the bureaucratic model replaces work with worship (arrow 4), for work falls outside the perimeter of orthodoxy and is regarded as a grey area – not entirely bad but not completely good either. It is left to the less spiritual "laity" and in the process, excludes work as an active agent for historically shaping the world. Therefore, bureaucracy must create its own virtual-reality where orthodox ideas can find expression. This is the function of worship. Here, sermons can be preached[392] without being interrupted by questions from the congregation. In an ordinary classroom setting, students are invited to ask questions for the clarification of ideas or for deliberation and debate. But raising such questions during a sermon would be regarded as improper. And that is the problem, worship is public and a common forum where the church could meet the world. But the world cannot ask questions in this forum; this contrasts with Jesus who taught in public and put up with all types of questions from the people, even with hecklers.

---

[392] The English word *preach* is normally used to translate the Greek verb *kerusso* (G2784) in the NT. *Kerusso* means to herald, announce or proclaim, LSJ. It implies the communication of something new and certainly not preaching to the converted.

Since work has no place in the bureaucratic model, goodness that originates from work vanishes. Orthodoxy replaces it with asceticism (arrow 5) and this becomes a manifestation of spirituality. But, it is an incomplete and non-biblical spirituality mostly focused on personal morality combined with religious practices such as prayer, meditation and participation in worship. The ascetic person practises self-denial for his own sake to make him feel more spiritual. However, the self denial that Jesus requires from his disciples is for the benefit of others. They are expected to carry a cross representing not their own problems, but the problems of the world. And he expects them to address their burden with more than mere charity. Charity is necessary but not sufficient, for it does not reach out with attempts to eliminate the causes that make charity necessary in the first place. Eliminating such causes requires reforming education, the economy, the use of technology, the health system and other such things. Things that an ascetic person relegates beyond the spiritual life.

Yet ascetic people are often serious people committed to their faith. Since this can best find expression within the church, they abandon what they regard as worldly pursuits to join the ranks of the clergy, become missionaries, nuns or monks depending on their church denomination. Asceticism then acts as a conduit to the church's bureaucracy (arrow 6) with the result that the leadership of the church is almost always in the hands of people who, due to their limited scope of Christianity cannot handle the problems of education, economics, health and technology. They close the loop formed by the arrows that connect bureaucracy => orthodoxy => asceticism => bureaucracy. This loop turns the church into a resilient and self-serving bureaucracy and keeps it in a steady equilibrium that is difficult to change, while outside of it the city burns.

Therefore, although the Early Fathers did not invent bureaucracy, they nevertheless became instruments in shaping the church into a rigid social structure that has withstood the times and even persecution. The conversion of the emperor Constantine and the gradual ascension of Christianity to being the official religion of Rome only strengthened its bureaucratic structure. It survived the fall of Rome and was able to convert the barbarians who took over. But, being only a religion and having only a religious agenda, it failed to civilise them and avoid the dark age that followed. The only threat to the church's bureaucracy came from the Christian Renascence and Reformation during the 16th and 17th centuries. Protestant theologians did not take long however, to stem the threat by holding firm to the division between laity and clergy and the strictly orthodox agenda of the church.

Neo-liberalism

We now turn to neo-liberalism – the spirit of our times– and examine the extent to which it has assimilated the bureaucratic model preserved by the church throughout the centuries. To do this, I have once again set two models side by side, the bureaucratic model on the left of Figure 12-2 and its neo-liberal equivalent on the right side. It is evident that the direction of the arrows in both models is similar to each other. I have also highlighted bureaucracy, the dominant form of social organisation in both models, as being the main trigger and determinant of the other socio-cultural factors. Although the other factors in the neo-liberal model have changed, they are only mutations of the earlier ecclesiastical factors.

While the neo-liberal bureaucracy professes to be secular, that is, it excludes belief in God, it does not exclude its own belief. Like Christianity, it has its own (godless) creed "Utility" (arrow 1) that must be accepted by faith much in the same way as Christians accept their creed. In the following litany, written by the neo-liberal, John Stuart Mill, he replaces God with happiness and calls the faithful to pursue it by stating:

> The creed which accepts as the foundation of morals, Utility, or the Greatest Happiness Principle, holds that actions are right in proportion as they tend to promote happiness, wrong as they tend to produce the reverse of happiness. By happiness is intended pleasure, and the

absence of pain; by unhappiness, pain, and the privation of pleasure.[393]

We must add to this that the pursuit of happiness is a purely
individualistic endeavour. Utility focuses on the individual experience of happiness, not on the happiness of the family, the
community or other social groups that are part of the social
fabric of humanity. The Utility creed pursues *my happiness,
my pleasure* and *my absence of pain* and ignores others. It assumes that these individual pursuits will lead by themselves to
the happiness of others, by the means of an "invisible hand"[394]
that, one assumes, replaces the hand of God.

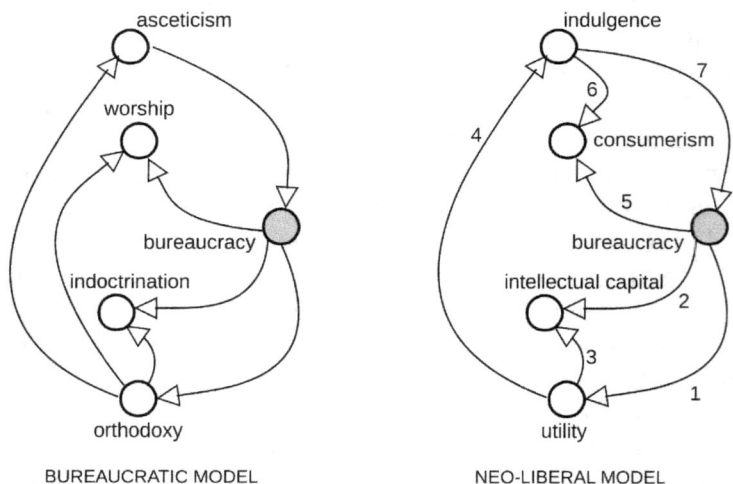

Figure 12-2: Mainstream Church and Neo-liberal Models

Since money[395] is the chief instrument of attaining the
Greatest Happiness, Utility becomes "profits" and those re-

---

[393] Mill, 2004, II. The basic idea behind utility originated in the 18th century with Adam Smith; it was further elaborated by Jeremy Bentham and
finally expressed as a creed by Mill in the 19th century.
[394] Smith, 1970, 4, II

sponsible for generating them are businesses[396]. They now occupy the place of the dominant bureaucracy – the place the church occupied prior to modernity – and they control every other institution, including the civil service, the political parties and the universities. The responsibility of the latter ones is also to make profits, so they have been turned into businesses that produce "intellectual capital" (arrow 2). Favourites among such intellectual capital are information technology[397], finance, marketing and business administration. The emergence of this has coincided with the demise of the humanities from the university syllabus[398]. Yet, it is the humanities – not the natural sciences – that teach people how to think. Without a grounding in the humanities, students are easily indoctrinated into an assembly line mentality that neatly fits them into the corporate factory as a human resource. To support this indoctrination by preaching Utility, neo-liberalism has assembled its own pulpit from the media, the press and the entire machinery of marketing. These not only shape the opinion of the man on the street, but also the syllabi of the university and the rest of the educational system (arrow 3).[399]

We must next consider the ethic that inspires the neo-liberal person. The creed of Utility states that the Greatest Happiness is found in satisfied pleasure. While both the old and new liberalism believe in the same creed, at the time the old liberalism emerged in the 18th century, Christian moral constraints were still firmly rooted in society. This limited the pursuit of pleasure dictated by the creed and kept it relatively confined. But with time, these moral constraints were gradually eroded and ultimately swept away when post-modernity made its entrance in the 1960s. When liberalism was resurrected in the 1970s,

---

[395] Neo-liberalism regards monetary policy as the most effective instrument to control the economy and generate wealth; see Friedman, 1968.

[396] According to the father of neo-liberalism, "the social responsibility of business is to increase its profits", Friedman, 1970.

[397] In proportion, modern information technology generates far more noise than information, J. D. R. de Raadt, 2015.

[398] Pan, 1998; Tapp, 1997; Engell, 1998

[399] J. D. R. de Raadt, 2016

the moral barriers that had hindered the pursuit of pleasure in the past were now removed. As a result, asceticism is now turned into its opposite, indulgence. Both are based on the same formula, but indulgence reverses the order of its variables. While asceticism is pain minus pleasure, indulgence, or the greatest happiness, is pleasure minus pain. Good is now determined by the amount of pleasure it produces (arrow 4).

We explained in Chapter 7 that asceticism and indulgence are symmetrical, that is, although opposed to each other, their impact draws every living creature away from a necessary stable equilibrium. Animals are protected from this through their environment. Thus, a predator is unlikely to suffer obesity because of the scarcity of prey on which it feeds. Moreover, catching prey requires a significant amount of exercise, which contributes to keeping the predator trim and healthy. People today have none of these environmental restraints, for they have been wiped off by scientific and technological advancement. But such lack of restraints do not translate into liberty as the word liberalism suggests. On the contrary, with neither moral nor natural barriers to halt his indulgence, man becomes a slave to his own instincts and emotions. He is at a disadvantage when compared to other living creatures, for rather than being surrounded by a constraining environment, businesses have created for him an environment made of malls, supermarkets, wholesale outlets and the like (arrow 5). Here he is irresistibly attracted by his indulgent spirit (arrow 6) in order to satisfy his every whim.

At the more extreme of the spectrum, businesses have taken advantage of the absence of mores and widened the scope of their products and services to satisfy more seamy forms of pleasure produced by sex and violence. Products and services in this sector include videos, films and computer games, rock concerts, seedy night clubs, sex shows and brothels. This has been accompanied by a campaign to undermine the moral perimeter of human sexuality and reproduction by legitimising prostitution[400], homosexual marriage and abortion on demand. At the same time, people who are opposed to such permissiveness are denigrated[401] and enormous pressure has been put on institutions to conform to relaxed standards of morality. For example, some medical information forms now ask a patient's "sexual orientation" in the same section that includes marital status rather than in the section that deals with health disorders. Australian government forms have done away with the term spouse and replaced it with "partner", meaning that the life commitment of marriage and the causal nature of partnership hold no difference before the justice system.

But the removal of moral boundaries is by no means over. Academics, based on the same philosophical argument that favours homosexuality and abortion, now support paedophilia and infanticide. Wilson, an Australian sociologist, backed paedophilia in these terms:

> I have argued that a legal age of consent is an arbitrary point, a line drawn that has no basis in the physiological or psychological development of the child...I would abolish any age of consent in sexual relations on the basis that in my opinion it is both unjust and unworkable, and I would also repeal all legislation relating to the age of consent in the field of sexuality specifically.[402]

---

[400] Brothels now employ "sex workers" and are listed in the stock exchange.

[401] An example of this is the word "homophobic" to describe people who disapprove of the practice of homosexuality. This term cynically turns the tables around. Rather than regarding homosexuality as a disorder, it regards objection to it – even if it is based on careful reasoning – as a psychological disorder.

[402] Wilson, 1981, Chapter 9. In 2016, Wilson has been described as a "celebrated criminologist, forensic psychologist, academic and author" who received the Order of Australia Medal in 2003. In 2016, he was sentenced to jail for sexually abusing a child under the age of twelve, Condon, 2016. A similar argument, under the euphemism of "intergenerational sex", has been advanced by Dowsett, 1982.

Likewise, Giubilini and Minerva supported infanticide as follows:

> If criteria such as the costs (social, psychological, economic) for the potential parents are good enough reasons for having an abortion even when the fetus is healthy, if the moral status of the newborn is the same as that of the infant and if neither has any moral value by virtue of being a potential person, then the same reasons which justify abortion should also *justify the killing of the potential person when it is at the stage of a newborn.*[403]

We should not dismiss these as outrageous ideas of some eccentric academics. We have already seen the path that such ideas follow from academia to a small group of activists, from activists to the media, from the media to the people and from the people to government policy. Given the naive susceptibility of modern man to swallow anything promoted by the media, it does not take long for these ideas to become the opinion of a majority of the public. It is the path followed by attitudes about abortion, LGBTI[404] or LGTBQ – terms that include almost any form of sexual practice – and same-sex-marriage. In

---

[403] 2012, p. 3, emphasis added

[404] In the state of Victoria, Australia, the department of education introduced a policy entitled "Safe Schools". It aims "to create an inclusive and safe environment for their school community, including for LGBTI students, families and teachers", Victoria State Government, n.d. This policy assumes that LGBTI represents normal patterns of behaviour, a view that is imposed upon students, families and teachers, without regard to their beliefs, moral convictions or the scientific basis of their objections. The policy dismisses any sociological or philosophical argument that indicates that LGBTI is a social and health disorder that needs to be treated as much for the general welfare of society as for the benefit of LGBTI people.

fact, political support of paedophilia[405] and post-birth abortion[406] have already sprung up in Europe. We may well ask, where is this all going to end? Is it possible that in the next decades, perhaps sooner, paedophilia and infanticide will become legal? What will happen to future generations? Will the "intellectual capital" they have acquired in university equip them to manage the social disaster that will loom upon them?

To satisfy their indulgence, people require money. This again makes them dependent on the bureaucracy, not as consumers, but now as employees (arrow 7). And that is the irony of neo-liberal man, although he thinks himself free to indulge his whims, he is indeed twice chained. Firstly, he is chained by unrestrained instincts that makes him obese or worse, an addict to drugs, gambling and other vices. Secondly, he is chained to an assembly line bureaucracy that removes him from family and community life. And upon all this looms the threat of unemployment, for businesses are constantly endeavouring to rid themselves of employees to cut costs and increase profits.

Employment, arrow 7, closes a loop linking the following factors: bureaucracy => utility => indulgence => bureaucracy. This loop is leading neo-liberal society to a gradual collapse[407] of which people seem painfully unaware. Their eyes are blinded by indulgence and the "idiot culture"[408] which has permeated modern life, the culture of a people who do not know how to think. Despite its pursuit of the "Greatest Happiness Principle", the neo-liberal society is not a happy one. We live

---

[405] Although a political party supporting paedophilia in the Netherlands was disbanded, it indicates that minorities will endeavour to promote their cause politically and it is possible that in the future such a party may re-emerge once it is able to gather the necessary signatures to register a candidate. In Germany, some members of the Green party have also been in favour to legalise paedophilia, see von Krempach, 2013.

[406] McCormack, 2013

[407] We have empirically researched the impact of these types of loops in communities in Sweden, Austria, France and Australia; these are described in detail in J. D. R. de Raadt and Veronica de Raadt, 2014.

[408] This expression was used by Bernstein, Associated Press, 2007; similar expressions conveying the same meaning have been used by other authors, see for example, Barber, 2007 and Díaz-Salazar, 1998.

in a world threatened by climate change and nuclear war[409]. The above loop adds to this global tension a local component of social fragmentation, unemployment, stress and the generation-gap produced by lack of responsible parenting and by the older generation's removal from the young people. Consumerism has proven to be more of an escape from unhappiness than a way to happiness.

The Emerging Church

Let us now turn to examine what has happened to the church in the midst of neo-liberalism and rampant secularism. Here we observe two responses. The first is displayed by the mainstream churches which remain stagnant by holding to their traditional models. The only change they have experienced is their shrinking congregations and consequent wane of their influence on society. The second response comes from a new branch of the church, known as "the emerging church". Like much of post-World War II culture, it is an import from the USA where the Utility creed is adhered to with quasi religious fervour.

The emerging church has done away with a sizeable portion of the long established theology, creeds and liturgy inherited from the mainstream churches. It considers the mainstream as outmoded and irrelevant to contemporary culture and seeks therefore to change its approach and become "culturally relevant". In practice, relevance means assimilating every aspect of neo-liberalism that does not clash with a narrowed-down Christian morality. This affords its members the best of both worlds; they can indulge in most of the pleasures of consumerism while at the same time remain in good standing before God.

Once again, to trace the influence of neo-liberalism on the emerging church, I have set their models next to each other in Figure 12-3. The organisation of most of these churches

---

[409] An ongoing monitoring of nuclear threat is carried out by the Bulletin of Atomic Scientists, n.d., and displayed in the "Doomsday Clock".

closely follows that of commercial businesses. Many of their senior pastors bear the additional title of "chief executive officer". Many also hold or are studying for an MBA degree. The creed promoted by emerging churches is commonly referred to as "prosperity gospel" (arrow 1). It is a subtle variation of the "Greatest Happiness Principle" and conveyed by some of the names that these churches have adopted. Examples of this are *The Happy Church*[410], *Enjoy Church*[411] and *The Fun Church*[412].

Happiness is seen as a blessing from God and closely connected to money generated by tithing. People who tithe are promised that God will bless them not only with health and happiness, but also with monetary gain several times the amount of their tithe, even "millions and billions of dollars"[413]. A large portion of the money from people's tithing is spent on lavish buildings, luxuries and large salaries enjoyed by pastors, similar to executives in other businesses. As may be expected, to finance its huge expenses, the sermons of the emerging church include a persistent call for tithing (arrow 2). They proclaim that the power of faith – of central importance to the prosperity gospel – can effortlessly produce anything. This makes thinking unnecessary and sermons an intellectual void (arrow 3). They leave the emerging Christian, especially the young ones, defenceless against the indoctrinating power of neo-liberalism and its intellectual capital. They are carried away along with the rest of society to indulge in the shopping malls (arrow 4).

But there are limitations that the emerging church must set over such indulgence; they mostly concern sex. As we have seen, the exploitation of the unrestrained sexual instinct, with the consequent destruction of marriage and family, is a powerful profit maker for neo-liberal businesses. In addition, the gratification of the sexual instinct functions also as a release

---

[410] <http://www.thehappychurch.org/>
[411] <https://enjoy.church/>
[412] <http://thefunchurch.org/>
[413] Lobdell, 2004

valve to the emotional tensions of bureaucratised modern living. Huxley explained this release thus:

> The society described in Brave New World is a world-state... where the first aim of the rulers is at all costs to keep their subjects from making trouble. This they achieve by (among other methods) legalizing a degree of sexual freedom (made possible by the abolition of the family) that practically guarantees the Brave New Worlders against any form of destructive (or creative) emotional tension.[414]

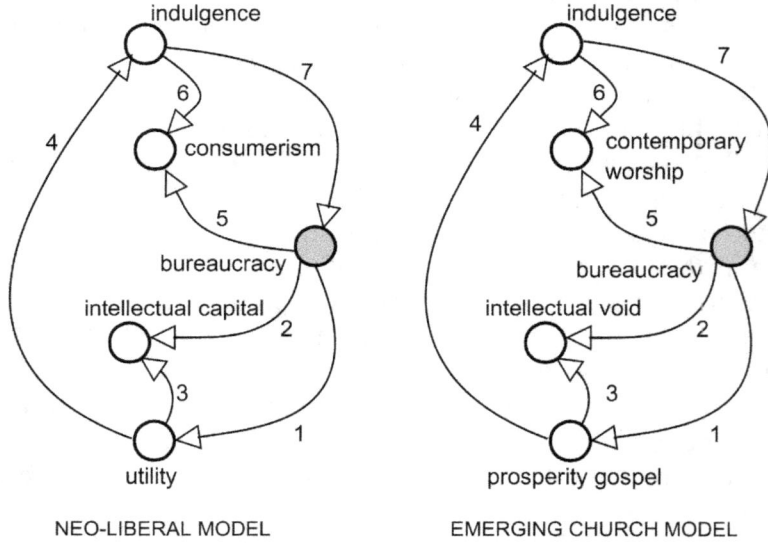

Figure 12-3: Neo-liberal and Emerging Church Models

Given that sexual freedom and the abolition of the family are in conflict with Christian teaching, the emerging church has provided an alternative release valve in "contemporary worship" (arrow 5). This type of worship is no longer conducted in a traditional church building but in a setting resembling

---

[414] 1965, III

a rock concert hall with the usual coloured lights, sound ampli-fiers and large video screens relaying enlarged images of the stage. Rather than releasing their "emotional tension" through sex, people in the audience express it by waving their arms, dancing, making meaningless sounds[415], laughing hysterically and collapsing on the floor (arrow 6). In addition to Sunday meetings, people may also gather at other times in smaller groups to engage in a "prayer bash".

Thus the emerging church has a twofold attraction to people to join its membership (arrow 7); it allows them to join non-Christians in consumerist indulgence and provides them with an emotional release in its version of contemporary worship. Arrow 7 closes a similar loop to the neo-liberal model that spans *bureaucracy => prosperity gospel => indulgence => bureaucracy*. Undoubtedly, this loop's potential to please has contributed to the steady growth in emerging church member-ship.

This completes our endeavour to explain how people have lost their social habitat made of family, community and work and how they have been penned in by bureaucracies. These, like a zoological garden, keep people fed and provided for, but in captivity. And like every captive creature, they have adapted to it and enjoyed, if they are privileged enough, the goods and services they consume in the same manner that a dog enjoys his bone and his walk. Both enjoyments, whether they are pro-duced by sophisticated or simple things, carry no further meaning beyond the instant gratification they produce.

Sadly, our task has been to uncover the roots of this zoolo-gical garden and to demonstrate that they lay buried in the post-apostolic period and have been carefully preserved over the centuries. Neo-liberal bureaucracy, along with other ex-pressions of modernity such as socialism, is largely an emula-tion of the church's model. The verdict is plain, the church has provided a model that has rendered people captives when its

---

[415] This is not the speaking in tongues mentioned in the NT, which carries a translatable and meaningful message, but simply the uttering of mean-ingless sounds to release emotion.

mission was to release them from such captivity[416]. Instead of providing release, one wing of the church – the mainstream – has reacted with stupor and disgust at the outrage of our times, but has been incompetent to put an end to it. The other, the "emerging" wing, has chosen to become relevant and joined in the neo-liberal revelry with the utmost gusto.

---

[416] Luke 4:18-19

13 Exodus from Bureaucracy

This book has been written for university students to avoid becoming bound by secular bureaucracy or the bureaucracy of the church, whether traditional or contemporary. We wish to encourage them to step out of the bureaucracy and to develop a new community, for one cannot put new wine in old skins[417]. We have laboured for decades to provide them with an educational programme that will equip them to do this. Being now retired from the university, we have dedicated this stage of our lives to write the textbooks which we would have liked to have had available when we lectured in the classroom. Naturally, we hope that they will be read. But there is, in addition, some practical advice, we would like to leave behind before closing. And that is: a good step towards community development is to enter into a solid marriage. Since there are people who are confused about what this is, I make it clear that I mean a covenant between a man and woman binding them:

> for better for worse, for richer for poorer, in sickness and in health, to love and to cherish, till death them do part, according to God's holy ordinance...[418]

and nothing else. The love and cherishing between husband and wife must then spread beyond them, first to their children and then to the people who surround them. The aim is to shape a community that is itself modelled on the family and characterised by justice, beauty and love. Let us not think that this is an over- idealistic agenda:

> A Christian family, living in a distinctively Christian style, is for cultural life, in whatever complications it may be placed, another revelation of the wholesome power for which one looks in vain in Hollywood...[419]

These words were not written by some utopian dreamer but by Klaas Schilder, a Dutch theologian[420] who lived during some

---

[417] Matthew 9:17
[418] Church of England, The Book of Common Prayer
[419] Schilder, 1977, p. 34
[420] This is an illustration of clergymen – mentioned in the introductory

of the darkest periods of Holland's history. He was arrested in 1940 for his political activities and for writing against National Socialism. He was well acquainted with the harsh treatment dealt to fighters against bureaucracy, especially of the dictatorial kind.

The road to social reform is narrow and stony[421]. It confronts us with an arduous journey and demands far more than personal morality and piety. Again, Schilder reminds us that:

> a quasi-edifying Pietism has all too often forgotten – and even branded as heresy – that the work of redemption leading us back to the "original" things imposes on the new man the duty of cultural labour.[422]

I think he means the sort of labour that demands competence in many sciences and philosophy. This is not the philosophy that merely satisfies overspecialised academic curiosity but rather the philosophy of Christ that binds all sciences together and articulates them in a manner that is beneficial to humanity and leads to the mastery of technology and its wise application.

Confronted with such an ominous task, what can motivate young people to the take up their cross and commence the painful task of removing the social debris of our times and replace it with something new? As I have often argued, only the Spirit of Christ can motivate them; there is no other alternative. This does not mean pursuing a mystical experience, but on the contrary, opening their eyes to what has always concretely stood before them: God's Creation both of nature and man. The Psalms beautifully paint the splendour of both. The earth is full of God's riches[423] and in its midst he has placed man crowned with glory and honour[424]. Despite all the pollution generated by man, both physical and cultural, the earth is still

---

chapter – who are able to broaden their scope beyond theology and redefine their work to serve best the needs of the laity.
[421] Matthew 7:13-14
[422] 1977, p. 45
[423] Psalm 104:24
[424] Psalm 8:5

a beautiful place to contemplate and in which to live and work. The flaming sword[425] that once barred man's passage to the tree of life has been removed by Christ[426], so we can now set ourselves to work to get all things back to their "original" condition. For both the earth and the work that serves humanity and honours the Creator will prevail.

The culture of Christ of which Schilder wrote and which comprises everything – music, architecture, paintings, literature, science, technology – and also the humble loaf of bread – belongs both to the present and the future. For the kingdom of God is in our midst but also at hand. The wonderful music of Bach, Bruckner and Sibelius which we can listen to today, we will also be able to listen to after our death. And we will also be able to admire Vermeer's paintings and the lace work of the girl who posed for him. This ought to be motivation enough for us all to roll up our sleeves and get on with our work with diligence and care in order to present it to God on the day of our departure from this world.

---

[425] Genesis 3:24
[426] Colossians 1:19-20

References

Artha Dictionary (2012)
<http://artha.sourceforge.net/wiki/index.php/Home>
(Accessed 27 July 2017).

Ashby, W. Ross (1976) *An Introduction to Cybernetics*.
London, Methuen.

Associated Press (2007) Carl Bernstein laments U.S.'s 'idiot
culture': Reporter raps media, reader infatuation with
celebrity news. *MSNBC.*
<http://www.msnbc.msn.com/id/21595196/> (Accessed 2
November 2007).

Barber, Benjamin R. (2007) *Consumed: How Markets Corrupt
Children, Infantilize Adults, and Swallow Citizens Whole.*
New York, Norton.

Beer, Stafford (1994) *Brain of the Firm.* (2nd. ed.) Classic
Beer Series. Chichester, Wiley.

Boulding, Kenneth E. (1956) General Systems Theory - The
Skeleton of Science. *Management Science*, 2: 197-208.
<http://www.panarchy.org/boulding/systems.1956.html>
(Accessed 15 October 2008).

Brent, Allen (2007) *Ignatius of Antioch: A Martyr Bishop and
the Origin of Episcopacy.* London, T&T Clark
International.

Bruce, F. F. (1970) *The Spreading Flame: The Rise and
Progress of Christianity from its First Beginnings to the
Conversion of the English.* Exeter, Paternoster.

Bulletin of Atomic Scientists (n.d.) Doomsday Clock.
http://thebulletin.org/doomsday-dashboard> (Accessed 29
July 2017).

Church of England (1662) *The Book of Common Prayer.*
<https://www.vulcanhammer.org/whats-important-in-
christianity/1662-book-of-common-prayer/> (Accessed 03
October 2016).

Condon, Matthew (2016) Celebrated Criminologist Paul

---

[427] All translations from original Spanish works are my own.
[428] Where available, I have provided references to digitalised versions in
the public domain and on the Internet.

Wilson's Fall from Grace. T*he Courier-Mail*, 24 November 24.
<http://www.couriermail.com.au/news/queensland/crime-and-justice/celebrated-criminologist-paul-wilsons-fall-from-grace/news-story/8e82bc210fca0c86a5a58ea8dfc27c0f> (Accessed 16 August 2017).

D'Souza, Albert (2005) *Christian Ethics and Moral Values*. New Dehli, India, Mittal.

de Beer, Wynand (2010) *The Platonist Christian Cosmology of Origen, Augustine, and Eriugena*. <http://unisouthafr.academia.edu/Departments/Religious_Studies_and_Arabic/Documents> (Accessed 23 May 2017).

de Raadt, J. D. R. (2000) *Redesign and Management of Communities in Crisis*. Parkland, Universal Publishers. <http://www.melbourneccd.com/download-books.html> (Accessed 26 February 2015).

de Raadt, J. D. R. (2001) *A Method and Software for Designing Viable Social Systems*. Parkland, Universal Publishers. <http://www.melbourneccd.com/publications.html> (Accessed 11 June 2014).

de Raadt, J. D. R. (2013) *Intelligent Christianity for an Age of Folly*. Melbourne, Melbourne Centre for Community Development. <http://www.melbourneccd.com/download-books.html> (Accessed 26 February 2015).

de Raadt, J. D. R. (2015) *Information and Managerial Wisdom*. Second Edition. Melbourne Centre for Community Development. <http://www.melbourneccd.org/books/imw.pdf> (Accessed 24 April 2016).

de Raadt, J. D. R. (2016) ¿Quo vadis? Where are the University and Science Going? *Systems Research and Behavioral Science*, 33:289-302. <http://www.melbourneccd.org/articles.html> (Accessed 07 September 2017).

de Raadt, J. D. R. and de Raadt, Veronica D. (2008) Arresting the Collapse of the City Through Systemic Education: A Case Study of Melbourne. *Systemic Practice and Action Research*, 21: 299-322. <http://www.melbourneccd.com/download-articles.html> (Accessed 26 February 2015).

de Raadt, J. D. R. and de Raadt, Veronica D. (2014) *From Multi-Modal Systems Thinking to Community Development*. Melbourne, Melbourne Centre for Community Development. <http://www.melbourneccd.com/books.html> (Accessed 26 February 2015).

de Raadt, Veronica D. (2002) *Ethics and Sustainable Community Development*. Parkland, Florida, Universal Publishers. <http://www.melbourneccd.com/download-books.html> (Accessed 26 February 2015).

Díaz-Salazar, Rafael (1998) *La Izquierda y el Cristianismo*. Madrid, Taurus.

Dowsett, Gary (1982) Boiled Lollies and Bandaids. *Gay Information*, Spring:34-38. <https://drive.google.com/file/d/0B9zGmvTCoD74RHhiN HVUa3BOc1k/view> (Accessed 19 September 2017).

Engell, James and Dangerfield, Anthony (1998) The Market-Model University. Humanities in the Age of Money. *Harvard Magazine*, May-June. <http://www.harvardmag.com/issues/mj98/forum.html> (Accessed 06 February 2013).

Erasmus, Desiderius (1529) *An Exhortation to the Diligent Study of Scripture*. Edited Frank Luttmer. <http://history.hanover.edu/courses/excerpts/346erasmus.ht ml> (Accessed 21 July 2008).

Field, Frederick (1875) *Hexapla*. 2 vols. Oxford, Clarendon. <https://archive.org> (Accessed 23 May 2017).

Friedman, Milton (1968) The Role of Monetary Policy. *The American Economic Review*, Vol. 58, No. 1. (Mar., 1968), pp. 1-17. <http://www.jstor.org/stable/1831652? seq=1#page_scan_tab_contents> (Accessed 11 August 2017).

Friedman, Milton (1970) The Social Responsibility of Business is to Increase its Profits. *The New York Times Magazine*, September 13.

Giubilini, Alberto and Minerva, Francesca (2012) After-birth abortion: why should the baby live? *Journal of Medical Ethics*. <http://jme.bmj.com/content/early/2012/03/01/medethics-2011-100411.full.pdf+html> (Accessed 20 July 2016).

Grau, Sergi (2011) Philosophy for the Body, Food for the Mind. *Coolabah*, 5, Australian Studies Centre, Universitat de Barcelona <http://www.ub.edu/dpfilsa/8campsgraucoola5.pdf> (Accessed 06 November 2016).

Harris, Laird R.; Archer, Gleason L. and Waltke, Bruce K. (1980) *Theological Wordbook of the Old Testament*. 2 Volumes. <http://www.theword.net/index.php?downloads.modules&group_id=5&o=title&l=english> (Accessed 04 March 2013).

Huxley, Aldous (1965) *Brave New World Revisited*. New York, Harper & Row.

Kerr, Hugh T. (Ed.) (1966) *Readings in Christian Thought*. Nashville, Tenessee, Abingdon.

Kohler, Kaufmann and Margolis, Max L. (1906) Celibacy. *Jewish Encyclopedia*. <http://www.jewishencyclopedia.com/articles/4166-celibacy> (Accessed 23 July 2016).

Kuyper, Abraham (1950) *Christianity and the Class Struggle*. Translated by Dirk Jellema. Grand Rapids, Michigan, Piet Hein. <http://www.reformationalpublishingproject.com/pdf_books/Scanned_Books_PDF/ChristianityandtheClassStruggle.pdf> (Accessed 15 October 2017).

Kuyper, Abraham (2000) *The Work of the Holy Spirit*. Christian Classics Ethereal Library. <http://www.ccel.org/ccel/kuyper/holy_spirit.pdf?membership_type=e21b214c09d19884c10c0f1bd9042d14151dc2ea> (Accessed 17 April 2008).

Liddell, Henry George; Scott, Robert (2011) *An Intermediate Greek English Lexicon* (Abridged). <http://www.theword.net/index.php?downloads.modules&group_id=5&o=title&l=english> (Accessed 04 March 2013).

Liddell, Henry George; Scott Robert; Jones, Henry Stuart (2009) *Lexicon of Classical Greek*. <http://www.theword.net/index.php?downloads.modules&group_id=5&o=title&l=english> (Accessed 04 March 2013).

Lobdell, William (2004) TBN's Promise: Send Money and See Riches. *Los Angeles Times,* 20 September. <http://www.latimes.com/local/california/la-na-tbn-gospel-pros-20160531-snap-htmlstory.html> (Accessed 31 July 2017).

Lu, Xiaohui (2008) Seventeenth-Century Dutch Genre Paintings of Women in the Household: The Case Study of Pieter de Hooch. BA Honours Thesis, University of Melbourne. <http://www.melbourneccd.com/articles/XiaHui.pdf> (Accessed 30 September 2017). (Accessed 30 September 2017).

Lyman, Rebecca (2009) Origen of Alexandria. *The Expository Times,* 120: 417-427.

McCormack, John (2013) Planned Parenthood Official Argues for Right to Post-Birth Abortion. *The Weekly Standard*, Florida, 29 March. <http://www.weeklystandard.com/video-planned-parenthood-official-argues-for-right-to-post-birth-abortion/article/712198> (Accessed 16 August 2017).

Mickelson, Jonathan Kristen (2015) *Enhanced Strong's Greek and Hebrew Dictionaries*. <http://www.theword.net/index.php?downloads.modules&group_id=5&o=title&l=english> (Accessed 22 February 2012).

Mill, J. S. (2004) *Utilitarianism*.

<http://www.gutenberg.org/ebooks/11224> (Accessed 17 July 2017).

Moore, Edward (n.d.) Origen of Alexandria. *Internet Encyclopedia of Philosophy*. <http://www.iep.utm.edu/origen-of-alexandria/> (Accessed 02 February 2017).

National Council of Churches of Christ, USA (1956) Paul Tillich in Conversation. Broadcast on the NBC-TV series Frontiers of Faith. <https://www.youtube.com/watch?v=56x_ZPrc0fQ> (Accessed 10 June 2017).

Origen (1957) *The Song of Songs Commentary and Homilies*, Translated by R. P. Lawson. London, Logmans.

Origen (n.d.) *On Prayer*. Translated by William A. Curtis. Christian Classics Ethereal Library. <http://www.ccel.org/ccel/origen/prayer.html> (Accessed 23 April 2017).

Ortega y Gasset, José (1924) *Kant - Hegel - Scheler*. <http://www.librodot.com> (Accessed 30 May 2008).

Ortega y Gasset, José (1996) *The Revolt of the Masses*. World Library. <http://www.19.5degs.com/ebook/revolt-of-the-masses/1419/read#list> (Accessed 23 April 2008).

Ortega y Gasset, José (2004) *Historia como Sistema: Sobre la Razón Histórica como Nueva Revelación*. <http://www.laeditorialvirtual.com.ar/Pages/Ortega_y_Gasset/Ortega_HistoriaComoSistema.htm> (Accessed 14 January 2012).

Pan, David (1998) The Crisis of the Humanities and the End of the University, *Telos*, 111: 69-106.

Philo Judaeus (1993) *The Works*. Translated by Charles Duke Yonge. <http://www.utom.org/library/books/Philo.pdf> (Accessed 8 November 2012).

Plato (1999) *Phaedo*. Translated by Benjamin Jowett. Pennsylvania State University, Electronic Classics Series. <http://www2.hn.psu.edu/faculty/jmanis/plato/phaedo.pdf> (Accessed 19 November 2012).

Plato (2008) *Timaeus and Critias*. Translated by Benjamin Jowett.

<https://ebooks.adelaide.edu.au/p/plato/p71ti/timaeus.html> (Accessed 09 February 2017).

Pliny (Ed. F. C. T. Bosanquet) (2013) *Letters of Pliny*. <http://www.gutenberg.org> (Accessed 18 August 2016).

Plotinus (2013a) *Complete Works, Volume 1*. <http://www.gutenberg.org> (Accessed 07 September 2017).

Plotinus (2013b) *Complete Works, Volume 2*. <http://www.gutenberg.org> (Accessed 07 September 2017).

Plotinus (2013c) *Complete Works, Volume 3*. <http://www.gutenberg.org> (Accessed 07 September 2017).

Plotinus (2013d) *Complete Works, Volume 4*. <http://www.gutenberg.org> (Accessed 07 September 2017).

Renwick, A. M. (1968) *The Story of the Church*. London, Intervarsity.

Richardson, Cyril C. (n.d.) *Early Christian Fathers*. <http://www.ccel.org/ccel/richardson/fathers.html> (Accessed 04 September 2017).

Rius-Camps, Josep (1977) Las Cartas Auténticas de Ignacio, el Obispo de Siria. *Revista Catalana de Teología*, 2: 31-149. <http://www.raco.cat/index.php/RevistaTeologia/article/vie wFile/65831/99503> (Accessed 14 July 2016).

Robles, Laureano Ed. (1996) *Miguel de Unamuno: Epistolario Americano* (1890-1936). Salamanca, España, Universidad de Salamanca.

Schaff, P. (Ed.) (n.d.a) *Ante-Nicene Fathers, Volume 1*. <http://www.ccel.org/ccel/schaff/anf01.pdf> (Accessed 05 March 2016).[429]

Schaff, P. (Ed.) (n.d.b) *Ante-Nicene Fathers, Volume 2*. <http://www.ccel.org/ccel/schaff/anf02.pdf> (Accessed 05 March 2016).

Schaff, P. (Ed.) (n.d.c) *Ante-Nicene Fathers, Volume 3*.

---

[429] In the notes citing Schaff, I have added the title of the specific work by the author; e.g., "Epistle to the Magnesians" in Note 128.

<http://www.ccel.org/ccel/schaff/anf03.pdf> (Accessed 05 March 2016).

Schaff, P. (Ed.) (n.d.d) *Ante-Nicene Fathers, Volume 4.* <http://www.ccel.org/ccel/schaff/anf04.pdf> (Accessed 05 March 2016).

Schaff, P. (Ed.) (n.d.e) *Ante-Nicene Fathers, Volume 5.* <http://www.ccel.org/ccel/schaff/anf04.pdf> (Accessed 05 March 2016).

Schaff, P. (Ed.) (n.d.f) *Ante-Nicene Fathers, Volume 9.* <http://www.ccel.org/ccel/schaff/anf09.pdf> (Accessed 06 March 2017).

Schilder, Klaas (1977) *Christ and Culture.* <http://www.contra-mundum.org/books/CandC.pdf> (Accessed 06 August 2017).

Smith, Adam (1970) *The Wealth of Nations.* Project Gutenberg. <http://www.gutenberg.org/dirs/etext02/wltnt10.txt> (Accessed 15 July 2008).

Tapp, Robert B. (1997) The Demise of the Humanities Department at the University of Minnesota. *Humanism Today*, 11. <http://www.humanismtoday.org/vol11/tapp.html> (Accessed 06 February 2013).

The Nag Hammadi Library (1984) *The Gospel of Truth.* Translated by Robert M. Grant. <http://gnosis.org/naghamm/got.html> (Accessed 18 November 2016).

Tillich, Paul (Ed. Carl E.Braaten) (1968) *A History of Christian Thought.* London, SCM.

Victoria State Government (n.d.) Education and Training - Safe Schools. <http://www.education.vic.gov.au/about/programs/health/Pages/safe-schools-coalition.aspx?Redirect=1#link30> (Accessed 23 September 2017).

von Krempach, J. C. (2013) The German "Green Party" Haunted by its Paedophile Past (and Present) <https://c-

fam.org/turtle_bay/the-german-green-party-haunted-by-its-paedophile-past-and-present/> (Accessed 16 August 2017).

Weber, Max (2009) *The Theory Of Social And Economic Organization* [Kindle Android version]. Retrieved from Amazon.com.

Wilson, Paul R. (1981) *The Man they Call Monster: Sexual Experiences Between Men and Boys.* North Ryde, New South Wales, Cassell. <https://www.ipce.info/host/wilson/> (Accessed 16 August 2017).

Index

www.ingramcontent.com/pod-product-compliance
Lightning Source LLC
Chambersburg PA
CBHW062201280526
45788CB00001B/395